HMH SCIENCE DIMENSIONS™
ENERGY & ENERGY TRANSFER

Module I

This Write-In Book belongs to

Sarah Quevedo

Teacher/Room

Garvey /201

Consulting Authors

Michael A. DiSpezio

Global Educator
North Falmouth, Massachusetts

Michael DiSpezio has authored many HMH instructional programs for Science and Mathematics. He has also authored numerous trade books and multimedia programs on various topics and hosted dozens of studio and location broadcasts for various organizations in the United States and worldwide. Most recently, he has been working with educators to provide strategies for implementing the Next Generation Science Standards, particularly the Science and Engineering Practices, Crosscutting Concepts, and the use of Evidence Notebooks. To all his projects, he brings his extensive background in science, his expertise in classroom teaching at the elementary, middle, and high school levels, and his deep experience in producing interactive and engaging instructional materials.

Marjorie Frank

Science Writer and Content-Area Reading Specialist
Brooklyn, New York

An educator and linguist by training, a writer and poet by nature, Marjorie Frank has authored and designed a generation of instructional materials in all subject areas, including past HMH Science programs. Her other credits include authoring science issues of an award-winning children's magazine, writing game-based digital assessments, developing blended learning materials for young children, and serving as instructional designer and coauthor of pioneering school-to-work software. In addition, she has served on the adjunct faculty of Hunter, Manhattan, and Brooklyn Colleges, teaching courses in science methods, literacy, and writing. For *HMH Science Dimensions*™, she has guided the development of our K–2 strands and our approach to making connections between NGSS and Common Core ELA/literacy standards.

Acknowledgments for Covers

Cover credits: (water wheel) ©HMH; (thermal image of iron) ©Joseph Giacomin/Cultura/Getty Images.

Section Header Master Art: (waves, computer artwork) ©Alfred Pasieka/Science Source.

Printed in the U.S.A.

ISBN 978-0-544-86104-6

13 0877 25 24 23 22

4500844102 A B C D E F G

Michael R. Heithaus, PhD

Dean, College of Arts, Sciences & Education
Professor, Department of Biological Sciences
Florida International University
Miami, Florida

Mike Heithaus joined the FIU Biology Department in 2003 and has served as Director of the Marine Sciences Program and Executive Director of the School of Environment, Arts, and Society, which brings together the natural and social sciences and humanities to develop solutions to today's environmental challenges. He now serves as Dean of the College of Arts, Sciences & Education. His research focuses on predator-prey interactions and the ecological importance of large marine species. He has helped to guide the development of Life Science content in *HMH Science Dimensions*™, with a focus on strategies for teaching challenging content as well as the science and engineering practices of analyzing data and using computational thinking.

Cary I. Sneider, PhD

Associate Research Professor
Portland State University
Portland, Oregon

While studying astrophysics at Harvard, Cary Sneider volunteered to teach in an Upward Bound program and discovered his real calling as a science teacher. After teaching middle and high school science in Maine, California, Costa Rica, and Micronesia, he settled for nearly three decades at Lawrence Hall of Science in Berkeley, California, where he developed skills in curriculum development and teacher education. Over his career, Cary directed more than 20 federal, state, and foundation grant projects and was a writing team leader for the Next Generation Science Standards. He has been instrumental in ensuring *HMH Science Dimensions*™ meets the high expectations of the NGSS and provides an effective three-dimensional learning experience for all students.

Program Advisors

Paul D. Asimow, PhD
Eleanor and John R. McMillan Professor of Geology and Geochemistry
California Institute of Technology
Pasadena, California

Joanne Bourgeois
Professor Emerita
Earth & Space Sciences
University of Washington
Seattle, WA

Dr. Eileen Cashman
Professor
Humboldt State University
Arcata, California

Elizabeth A. De Stasio, PhD
Raymond J. Herzog Professor of Science
Lawrence University
Appleton, Wisconsin

Perry Donham, PhD
Lecturer
Boston University
Boston, Massachusetts

Shila Garg, PhD
Emerita Professor of Physics
Former Dean of Faculty & Provost
The College of Wooster
Wooster, Ohio

Tatiana A. Krivosheev, PhD
Professor of Physics
Clayton State University
Morrow, Georgia

Mark B. Moldwin, PhD
Professor of Space Sciences and Engineering
University of Michigan
Ann Arbor, Michigan

Ross H. Nehm
Stony Brook University (SUNY)
Stony Brook, NY

Kelly Y. Neiles, PhD
Assistant Professor of Chemistry
St. Mary's College of Maryland
St. Mary's City, Maryland

John Nielsen-Gammon, PhD
Regents Professor
Department of Atmospheric Sciences
Texas A&M University
College Station, Texas

Dr. Sten Odenwald
Astronomer
NASA Goddard Spaceflight Center
Greenbelt, Maryland

Bruce W. Schafer
Executive Director
Oregon Robotics Tournament & Outreach Program
Beaverton, Oregon

Barry A. Van Deman
President and CEO
Museum of Life and Science
Durham, North Carolina

Kim Withers, PhD
Assistant Professor
Texas A&M University-Corpus Christi
Corpus Christi, Texas

Adam D. Woods, PhD
Professor
California State University, Fullerton
Fullerton, California

Classroom Reviewers

Cynthia Book, PhD
John Barrett Middle School
Carmichael, California

Katherine Carter, MEd
Fremont Unified School District
Fremont, California

Theresa Hollenbeck, MEd
Winston Churchill Middle School
Carmichael, California

Kathryn S. King
Science and AVID Teacher
Norwood Jr. High School
Sacramento, California

Donna Lee
Science/STEM Teacher
Junction Ave. K8
Livermore, California

Rebecca S. Lewis
Science Teacher
North Rockford Middle School
Rockford, Michigan

Bryce McCourt
8th Grade Science Teacher/Middle School Curriculum Chair
Cudahy Middle School
Cudahy, Wisconsin

Sarah Mrozinski
Teacher
St. Sebastian School
Milwaukee, Wisconsin

Raymond Pietersen
Science Program Specialist
Elk Grove Unified School District
Elk Grove, California

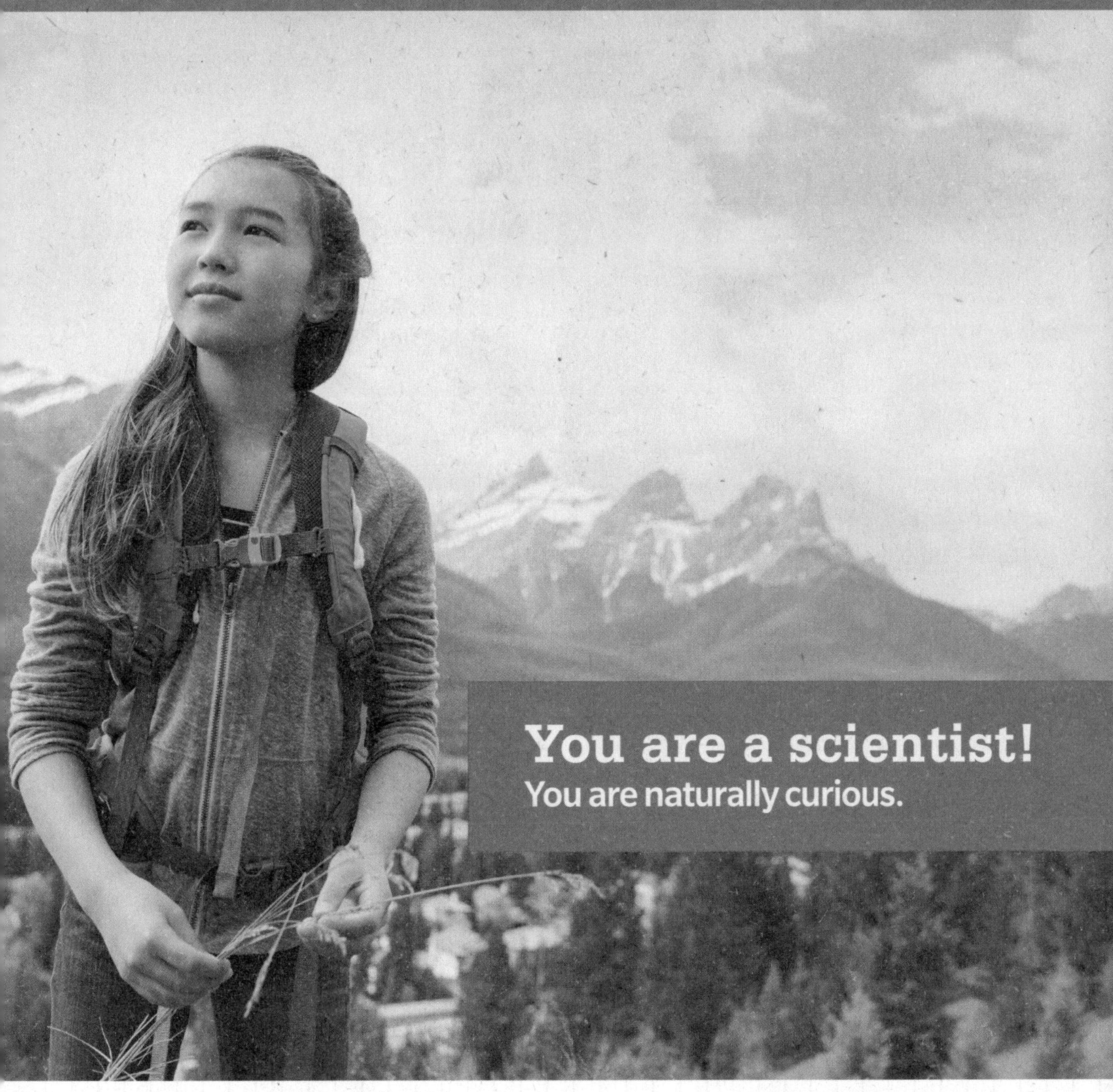

You are a scientist!

You are naturally curious.

Have you ever wondered . . .

- why is it difficult to catch a fly?
- how a new island can appear in an ocean?
- how to design a great tree house?
- how a spacecraft can send messages across the solar system?

HMH SCIENCE DIMENSIONS™
will *SPARK* your curiosity!

AND prepare you for

✓	tomorrow
✓	next year
✓	college or career
✓	life!

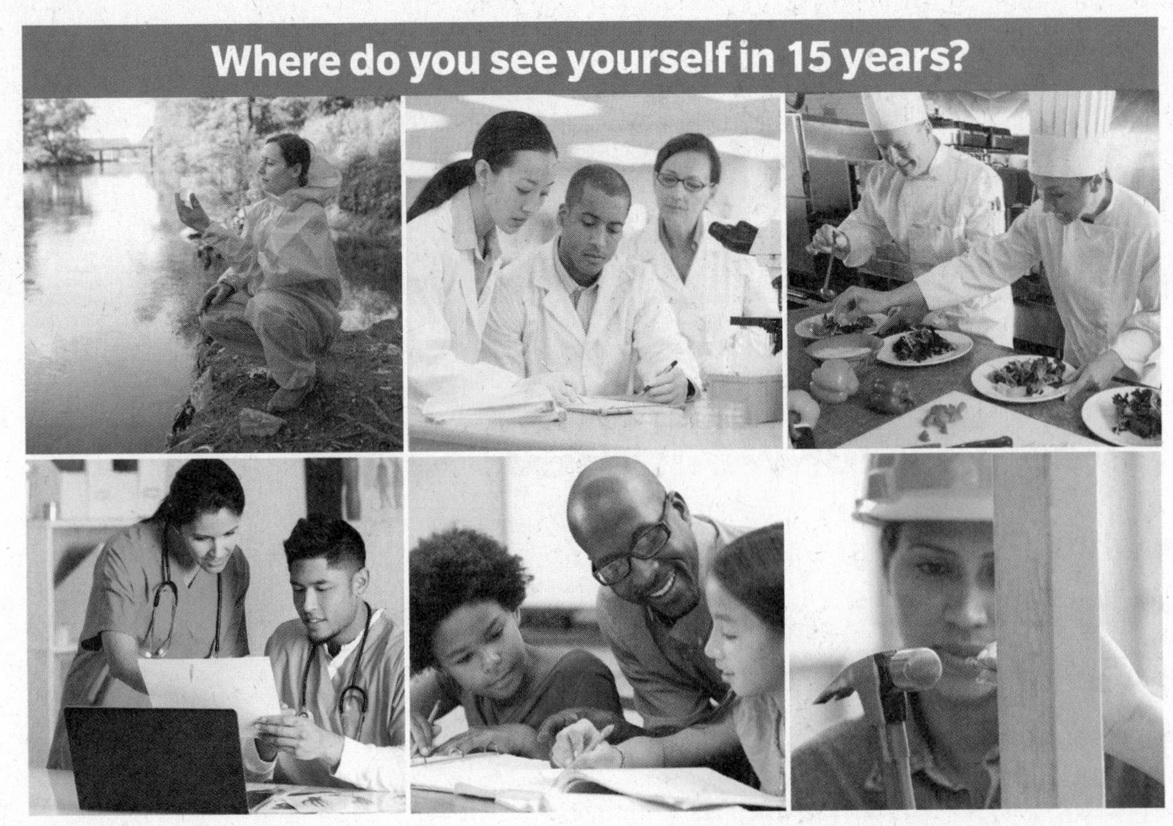
Where do you see yourself in 15 years?

Observe

Collect Data

Be a scientist.

Work like real scientists work.

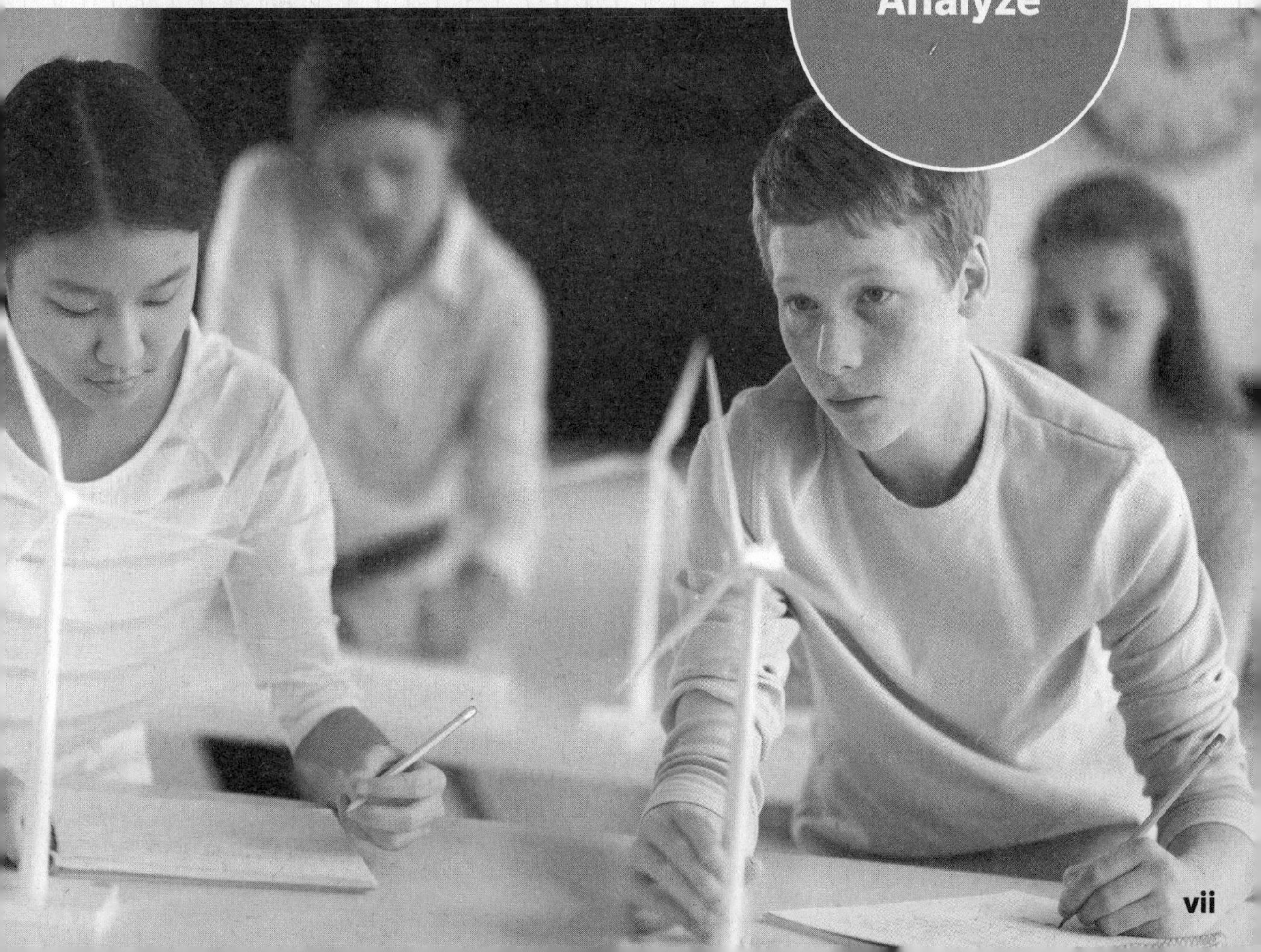

Analyze

Be an engineer.

Solve problems like engineers do.

Define Problems

Test Solutions

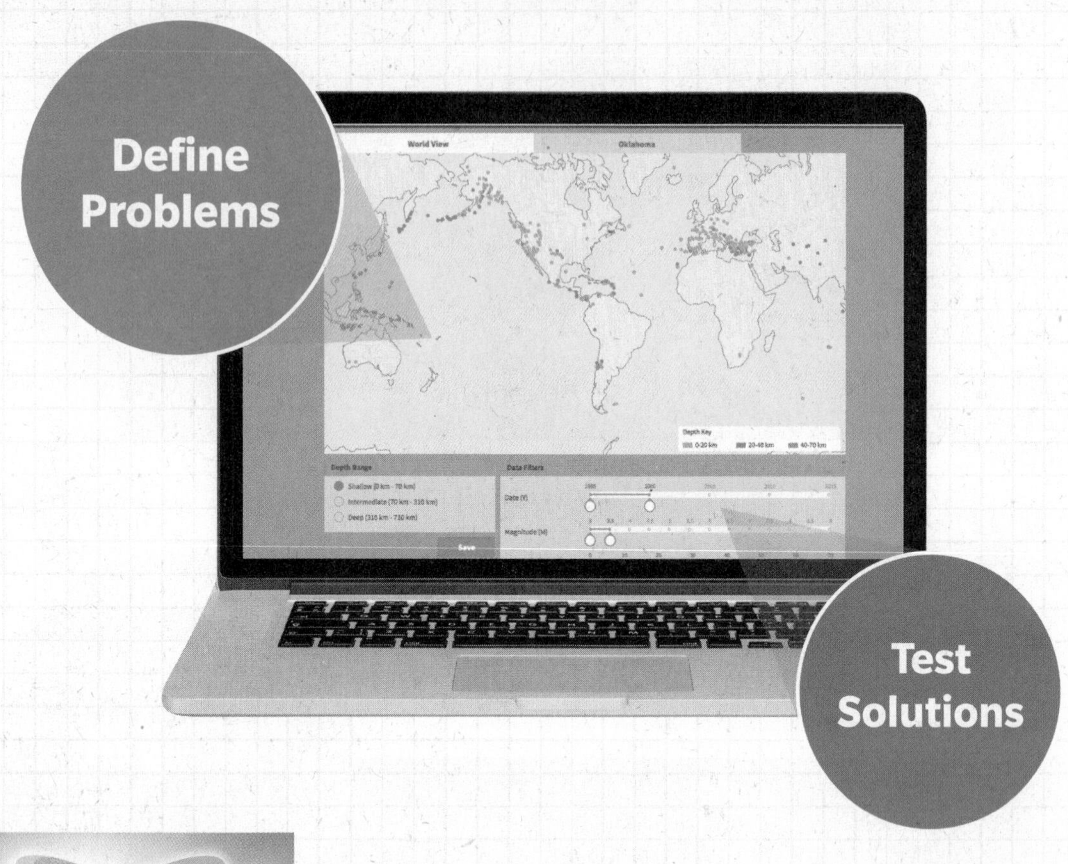

STEM

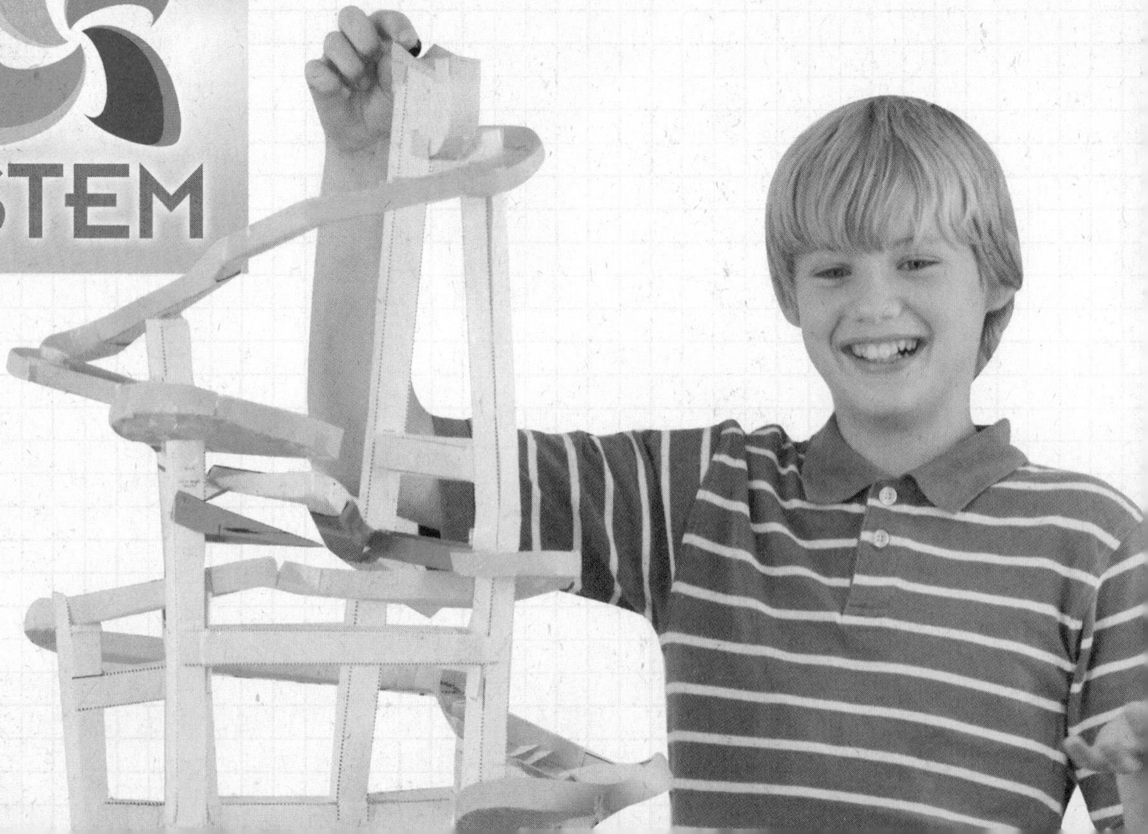

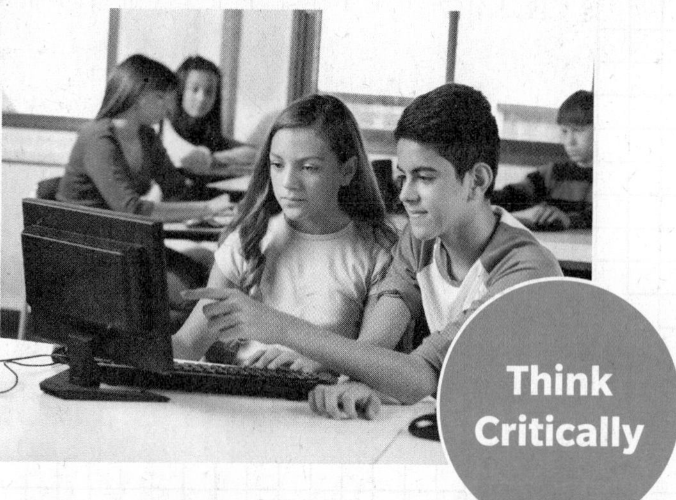

Explain your world.

Start by asking questions.

Conduct
Investigations

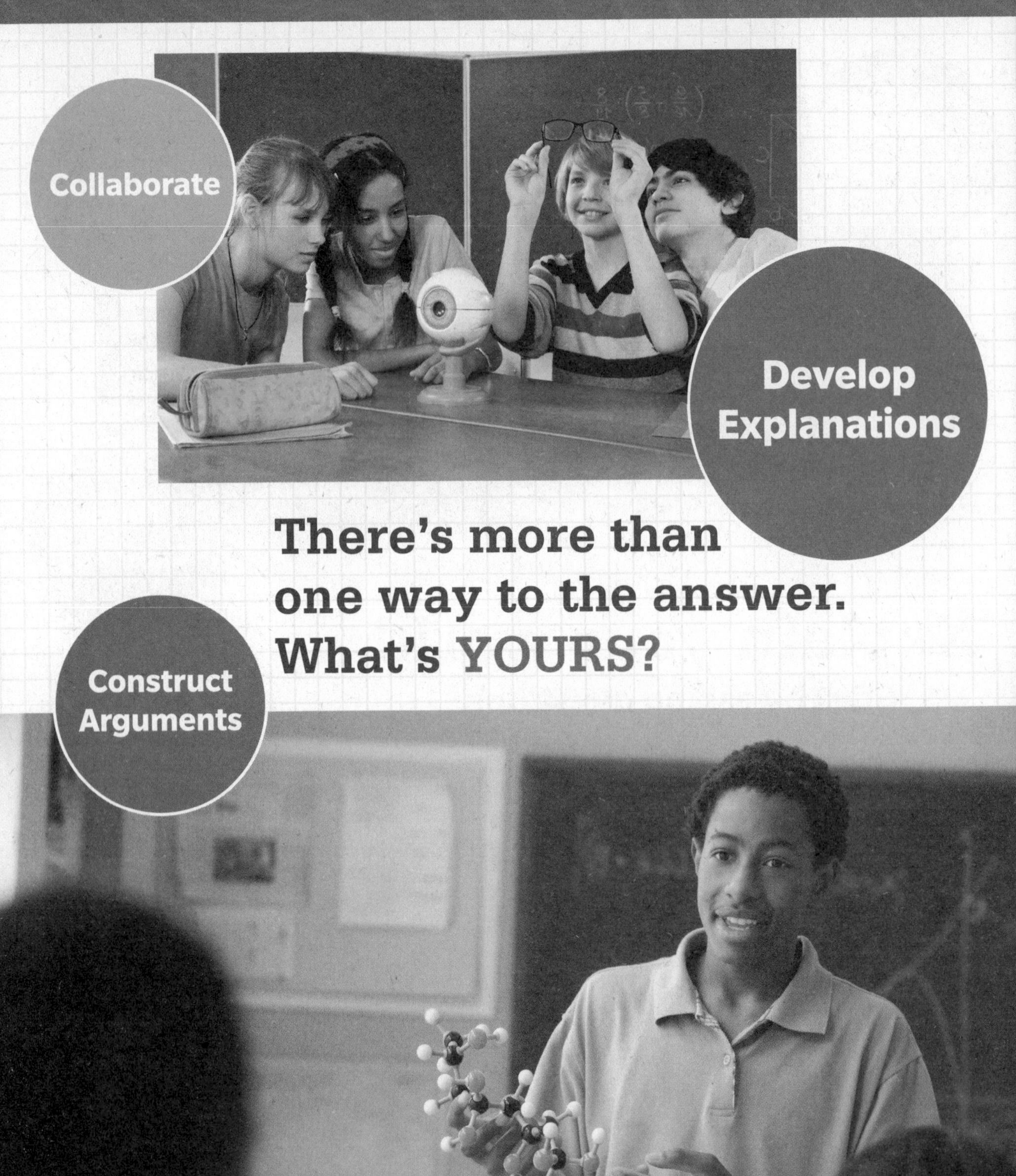

There's more than one way to the answer. What's YOURS?

YOUR Program

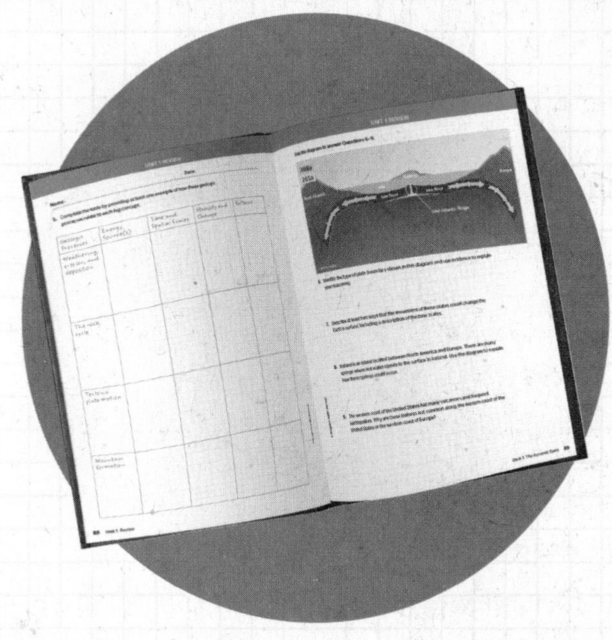

Write-In Book:

- a brand-new and innovative textbook that will guide you through your next generation curriculum, including your hands-on lab program

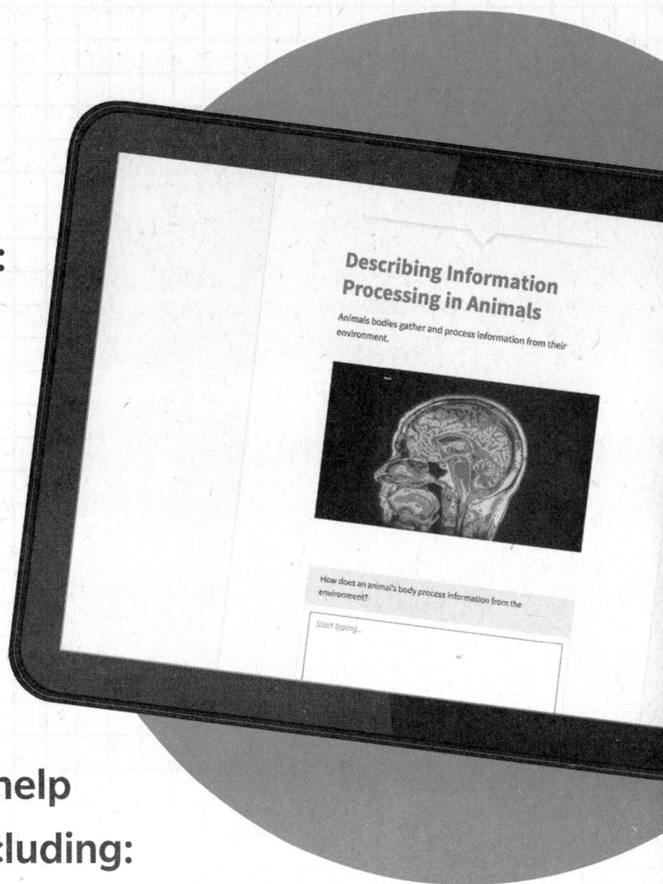

Interactive Online Student Edition:

- a complete online version of your textbook enriched with videos, interactivities, animations, simulations, and room to enter data, draw, and store your work

More tools are available online to help you practice and learn science, including:

- Hands-On Labs
- Science and Engineering Practices Handbook
- Crosscutting Concepts Handbook
- English Language Arts Handbook
- Math Handbook

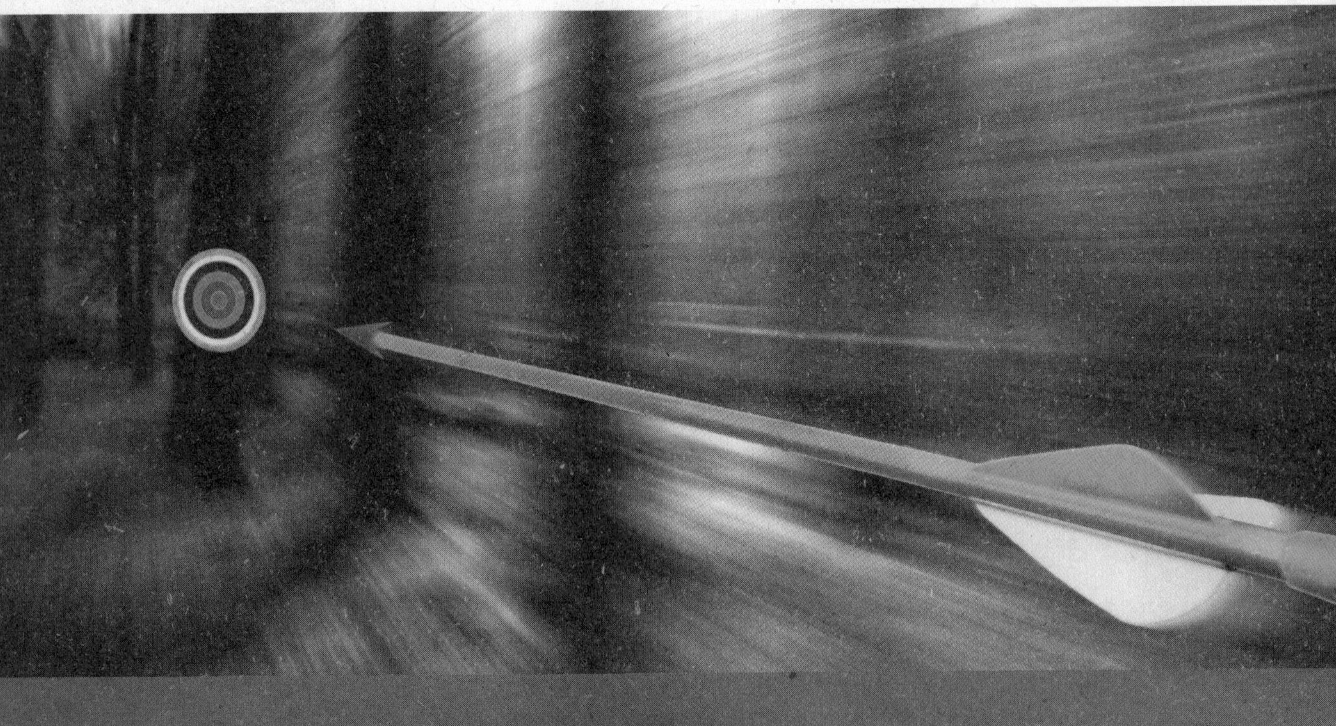

After an arrow is shot from a bow, it will fly through the air.

UNIT 2 69

Energy Transfer

Without energy inputs, the buildings will cool down to the ambient temperature.

Whether you are in the lab or in the field, you are responsible for your own safety and the safety of others. To fulfill these responsibilities and avoid accidents, be aware of the safety of your classmates as well as your own safety at all times. Take your lab work and fieldwork seriously, and behave appropriately. Elements of safety to keep in mind are shown below and on the following pages.

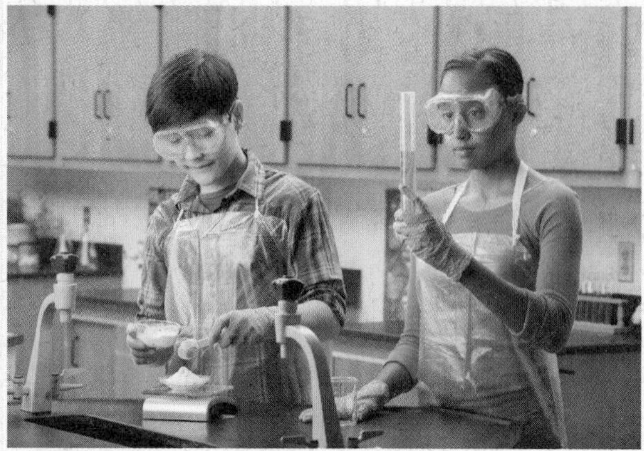

Safety in the Lab

- ☐ Be sure you understand the materials, your procedure, and the safety rules before you start an investigation in the lab.
- ☐ Know where to find and how to use fire extinguishers, eyewash stations, shower stations, and emergency power shutoffs.
- ☐ Use proper safety equipment. Always wear personal protective equipment, such as eye protection and gloves, when setting up labs, during labs, and when cleaning up.
- ☐ Do not begin until your teacher has told you to start. Follow directions.
- ☐ Keep the lab neat and uncluttered. Clean up when you are finished. Report all spills to your teacher immediately. Watch for slip/fall and trip/fall hazards.
- ☐ If you or another student are injured in any way, tell your teacher immediately, even if the injury seems minor.
- ☐ Do not take any food or drink into the lab. Never take any chemicals out of the lab.

Safety in the Field

- ☐ Be sure you understand the goal of your fieldwork and the proper way to carry out the investigation before you begin fieldwork.
- ☐ Use proper safety equipment and personal protective equipment, such as eye protection, that suits the terrain and the weather.
- ☐ Follow directions, including appropriate safety procedures as provided by your teacher.
- ☐ Do not approach or touch wild animals. Do not touch plants unless instructed by your teacher to do so. Leave natural areas as you found them.
- ☐ Stay with your group.
- ☐ Use proper accident procedures, and let your teacher know about a hazard in the environment or an accident immediately, even if the hazard or accident seems minor.

Safety Symbols

To highlight specific types of precautions, the following symbols are used throughout the lab program. Remember that no matter what safety symbols you see within each lab, all safety rules should be followed at all times.

Dress Code

- Wear safety goggles (or safety glasses as appropriate for the activity) at all times in the lab as directed. If chemicals get into your eye, flush your eyes immediately for a minimum of 15 minutes.
- Do not wear contact lenses in the lab.
- Do not look directly at the sun or any intense light source or laser.

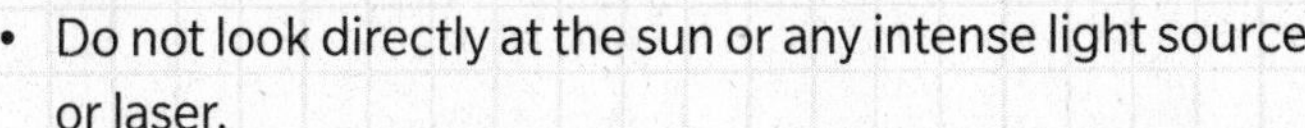

- Wear appropriate protective non-latex gloves as directed.
- Wear an apron or lab coat at all times in the lab as directed.
- Tie back long hair, secure loose clothing, and remove loose jewelry. Remove acrylic nails when working with active flames.
- Do not wear open-toed shoes, sandals, or canvas shoes in the lab.

Glassware and Sharp Object Safety

- Do not use chipped or cracked glassware.
- Use heat-resistant glassware for heating or storing hot materials.
- Notify your teacher immediately if a piece of glass breaks.
- Use extreme care when handling any sharp or pointed instruments.

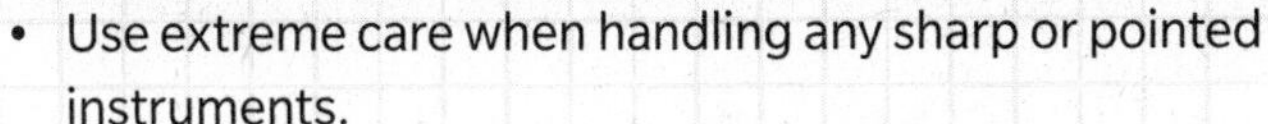

- Do not cut an object while holding the object unsupported in your hands. Place the object on a suitable cutting surface, and always cut in a direction away from your body.

Chemical Safety

- If a chemical gets on your skin, on your clothing, or in your eyes, rinse it immediately for a minimum of 15 minutes (using the shower, faucet, or eyewash station), and alert your teacher.
- Do not clean up spilled chemicals unless your teacher directs you to do so.
- Do not inhale any gas or vapor unless directed to do so by your teacher. If you are instructed to note the odor of a substance, wave the fumes toward your nose with your hand. This is called wafting. Never put your nose close to the source of the odor.
- Handle materials that emit vapors or gases in a well-ventilated area.
- Keep your hands away from your face while you are working on any activity.

Safety Symbols, continued

Electrical Safety

- Do not use equipment with frayed electrical cords or loose plugs.
- Do not use electrical equipment near water or when clothing or hands are wet.
- Hold the plug housing when you plug in or unplug equipment. Do not pull on the cord.
- Use only GFI-protected electrical receptacles.

Heating and Fire Safety

- Be aware of any source of flames, sparks, or heat (such as flames, heating coils, or hot plates) before working with any flammable substances.
- Know the location of the lab's fire extinguisher and fire-safety blankets.
- Know your school's fire-evacuation routes.
- If your clothing catches on fire, walk to the lab shower to put out the fire. Do not run.
- Never leave a hot plate unattended while it is turned on or while it is cooling.
- Use tongs or appropriately insulated holders when handling heated objects.
- Allow all equipment to cool before storing it.

Plant and Animal Safety

- Do not eat any part of a plant.
- Do not pick any wild plant unless your teacher instructs you to do so.
- Handle animals only as your teacher directs.
- Treat animals carefully and respectfully.
- Wash your hands throughly with soap and water after handling any plant or animal.

Cleanup

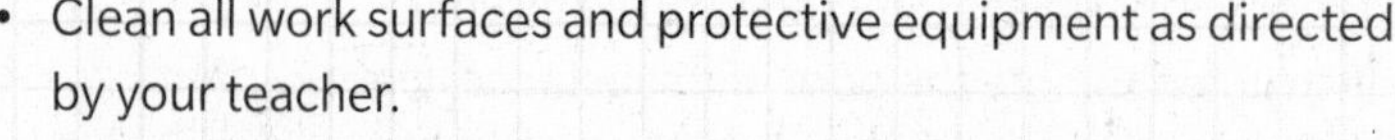

- Clean all work surfaces and protective equipment as directed by your teacher.

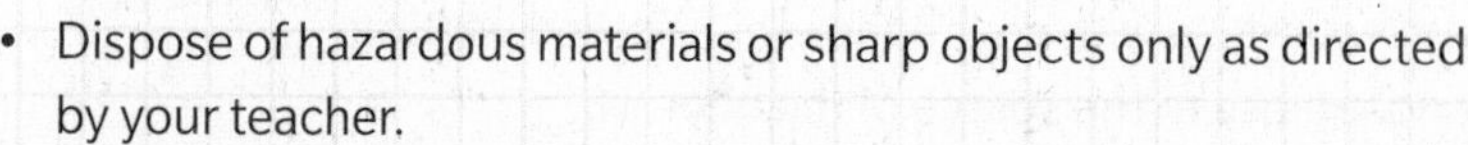

- Dispose of hazardous materials or sharp objects only as directed by your teacher.
- Wash your hands throughly with soap and water before you leave the lab or after any activity.

Name: Date:

Student Safety Quiz

Circle the letter of the BEST answer.

1. Before starting an investigation or lab procedure, you should
   A. try an experiment of your own
   B. open all containers and packages
   C. read all directions and make sure you understand them
   D. handle all the equipment to become familiar with it

2. At the end of any activity you should
   A. wash your hands thoroughly with soap and water before leaving the lab
   B. cover your face with your hands
   C. put on your safety goggles
   D. leave hot plates switched on

3. If you get hurt or injured in any way, you should
   A. tell your teacher immediately
   B. find bandages or a first aid kit
   C. go to your principal's office
   D. get help after you finish the lab

4. If your glassware is chipped or broken, you should
   A. use it only for solid materials
   B. give it to your teacher for recycling or disposal
   C. put it back into the storage cabinet
   D. increase the damage so that it is obvious

5. If you have unused chemicals after finishing a procedure, you should
   A. pour them down a sink or drain
   B. mix them all together in a bucket
   C. put them back into their original containers
   D. dispose of them as directed by your teacher

6. If electrical equipment has a frayed cord, you should
   A. unplug the equipment by pulling the cord
   B. let the cord hang over the side of a counter or table
   C. tell your teacher about the problem immediately
   D. wrap tape around the cord to repair it

7. If you need to determine the odor of a chemical or a solution, you should
   A. use your hand to bring fumes from the container to your nose
   B. bring the container under your nose and inhale deeply
   C. tell your teacher immediately
   D. use odor-sensing equipment

8. When working with materials that might fly into the air and hurt someone's eye, you should wear
   A. goggles
   B. an apron
   C. gloves
   D. a hat

9. Before doing experiments involving a heat source, you should know the location of the
   A. door
   B. window
   C. fire extinguisher
   D. overhead lights

10. If you get chemicals in your eye you should
   A. wash your hands immediately
   B. put the lid back on the chemical container
   C. wait to see if your eye becomes irritated
   D. use the eyewash station right away, for a minimum of 15 minutes

Go online to view the Lab Safety Handbook for additional information.

Energy

Solar flares are giant explosions on the surface of the sun. These flares send large amounts of electromagnetic energy toward Earth.

Energy is essential for life and all other processes on Earth. The sun is the main source of the energy that drives processes such as the production of food, weather systems, and even listening to music. Just what is energy? How do scientists describe different forms of energy? In this unit, you will learn how scientists and engineers classify energy and describe its relationship to matter.

Why It Matters

Here are some questions to consider as you work through the unit. Can you answer any of the questions now? Revisit these questions at the end of the unit to apply what you discover.

Questions	Notes
What do we mean when we say something is "doing work"?	
How does the potential energy of an object change as its distance from the ground changes?	
When have you experienced an increase in kinetic energy within a system?	
What are some examples of the application of chemical energy in an everyday technology?	
How many forms of energy associated with a computer can you describe?	

Unit Starter: Comparing Scale and Proportion

Think about how much effort is required to move these items. Use the photos to answer the questions.

1. The tractor-trailer requires more / less energy to move an equal distance as the small car.

2. If you were to lift the stack of books, you would do more / less work than someone lifting the single book the same amount.

Unit Project

Go online to download the Unit Project Worksheet to help you plan your project.

Roller Coaster Engineer

Roller coasters are thrilling and fun, but they require the precise application of scientific and engineering principles in order to function properly. Use your knowledge of energy and its interactions to design and build a model roller coaster.

LESSON 1

Introduction to Energy

This steam locomotive transforms energy from fuel into energy to propel it forward and transfers energy to the train cars it pulls.

By the end of this lesson . . .

you will be able to describe how energy interacts with and changes objects.

Go online to view the digital version of the Hands-On Lab for this lesson and to download additional lab resources.

CAN YOU EXPLAIN IT?

How is the energy from the first domino able to topple the last domino?

A domino chain reaction occurs when a series of dominoes is toppled after the first domino is knocked over. Each domino is able to topple another domino that is about 1.5 times larger than itself.

1. Think about the chain of dominoes as a system. What are the system's inputs and outputs?

2. How is the process started by the tiny domino at the beginning of the chain able to result in the toppling of the giant domino at the end of the chain?

EVIDENCE NOTEBOOK As you explore the lesson, gather evidence to help explain how energy flows through the domino system.

Analyzing Energy

If you look at the news or read an article today, you are likely to see a conversation about energy. Whether it is a question of renewable energy, energy conservation, or cost, the ways we obtain and use energy are some of the most important issues facing us in the 21st century. Engineers, scientists, and policymakers are busy looking for solutions for how we generate, distribute, and store energy.

The word *energy* is used in many contexts, but what does it actually mean? Scientists define **energy** as the ability to do work or to cause changes in matter. This ability to do work can be observed in examples as simple as a traditional wind-up toy or as complex as a crane lifting steel beams to construct a skyscraper. In both situations, the objects move because energy is added to them. Think about the operation of a wind-up toy. The user turns a key that tightly coils a spring. The energy stored in the spring is released as it unwinds, exerting a force on gears in the toy that cause it to move. The motion of the toy is the result of an initial input of energy from the user turning the key.

After the user winds the toy up with its key, the toy begins to move.

3. **Discuss** Think about a construction crane moving a steel beam. Where does the energy used to complete the task come from? What evidence do you have that the energy involved in the crane example is different from that in the wind-up toy example?

Energy and Work

In both a wind-up toy and a crane, a force applied to an object results in its movement over a distance. The amount of energy required to move a large steel beam over a specific distance is much greater than the energy needed to move a wind-up a toy an equivalent distance. This energy can be scientifically measured in terms of *work*. In science, **work** is defined as the transfer of energy to an object by a force that causes the object to move in the direction of that force.

Work (W) can be calculated using the formula $W = Fd$, where F is the force applied to the object and d is the distance the object moved. Force is in units of newtons (N), and distance is in units of meters (m), so work is defined in units of newton-meters (N•m), also known as joules (J). Note that if the object does not move, $d = 0$ and no work is done. Just how much is a joule of work? To get an idea, lift an apple (which weighs about one newton) from your feet to your waist (which is about one meter).

4. Do the Math Use the equation for work ($W = Fd$) to calculate the work done by each robot, and record the value in the space provided.

Robot 1 applies 20 N of force to lift 2 building blocks 3 m.

Robot 2 applies 30 N of force to lift 3 building blocks 3 m.

Robot 3 applies 10 N of force to lift 1 building block 2 m.

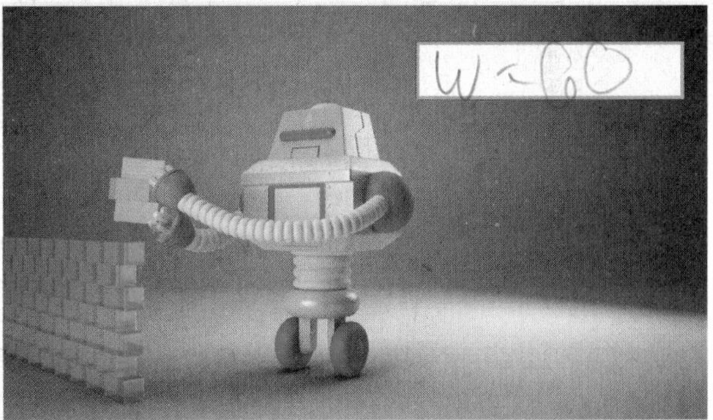

Robot 4 applies 30 N of force to lift 3 building blocks 2 m.

5. Which robot did the greatest amount of work? Which robot did the least amount of work? Which robots did the same amount of work?

In science and engineering, energy and work are related. Energy is the ability to do work, and work requires a transfer of energy. In fact, energy is transferred every time work is done. As the robots move the building blocks, they do work on the blocks by transferring energy from themselves to the blocks. Energy and work are both measured in joules (J).

6. **Language SmArts** You have probably heard the terms *energy* and *work* used in everyday contexts that are different from the scientific definitions of the words. Explain the differences between the everyday and the scientific uses of the terms *energy* and *work*. Create a visual aid to help explain the differences.

Potential and Kinetic Energy

As you have observed, every moving object requires energy to set it in motion. The more massive the object or the faster it is traveling, the more energy it has. This energy of motion is called **kinetic energy**. An object may also have stored energy based on its relative position within a system or its condition, known as **potential energy**. A roller coaster car at the top of a hill has stored energy that gives it the potential to move down the hill. The energy stored in an object due to its physical position and the force of gravity acting on it is called *gravitational potential energy*.

Potential energy can be transformed into kinetic energy and back again. Think about a rolling marble. If the marble is at the top of a ramp, it has gravitational potential energy because of its position above the floor. As the marble rolls down the ramp, it gains kinetic energy. At the bottom, nearly all of the potential energy has been transformed into kinetic energy. That kinetic energy can be transformed back into potential energy if the marble continues up another ramp.

7. In your neighborhood, people are setting up a downhill soapbox derby race. As a safety measure, bales of hay are set up at the bottom of the hill as a barricade to stop cars and drivers. At what point on the car's path will it have the most kinetic energy?
   A. at the very top of the hill
   B. at the midpoint of the hill
   C. at the very bottom of the hill
   D. after it collides with the hay

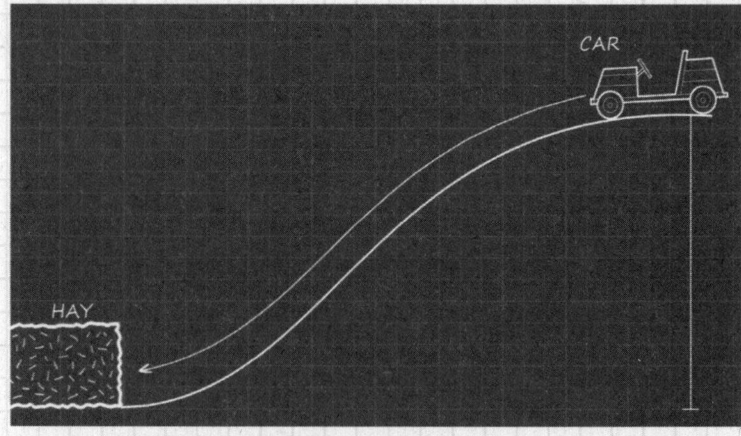

The bales of hay are placed at the bottom of the hill to stop a car and driver.

8. Engineer It Your job is to design the barricade for the downhill soapbox derby. How might your design need to change if heavier cars were used?

Forms of Energy

There are many forms of energy in the simple scene below. You can't see it, but the people in the photo are probably digesting food (chemical energy) to get the energy to throw the ball. The scene is illuminated by light (electromagnetic energy) from the sun. The waves are likely making noise (sound energy) as they crash. The ball and the waves have mechanical energy.

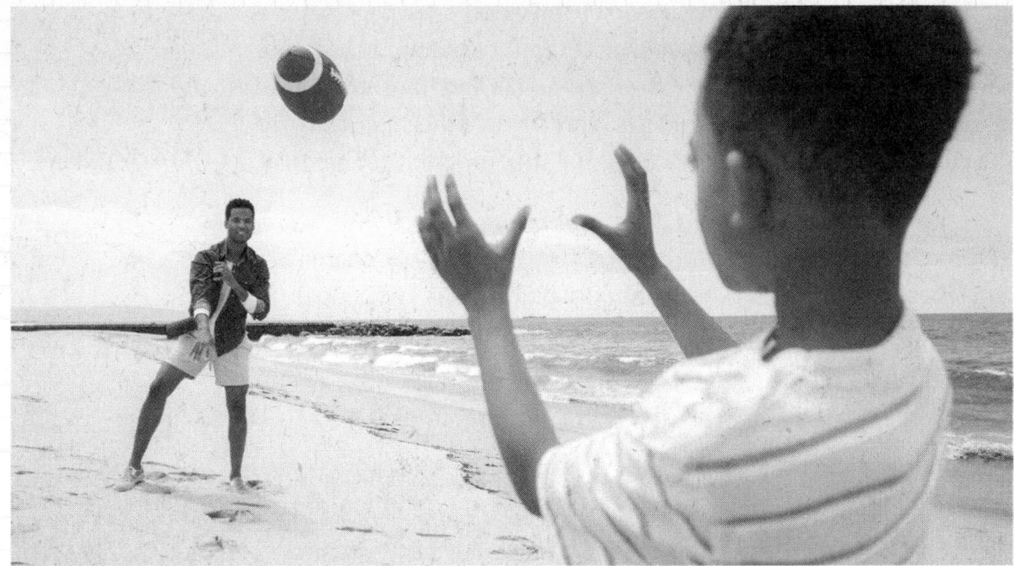

The ball has kinetic energy as it flies through the air. It also has gravitational potential energy because of gravity and its position above the ground.

Mechanical Energy The mechanical energy of an object is the sum of the object's kinetic energy and potential energy. In other words, mechanical energy is the energy of an object due to its motion and its position. A ball that flies through the air has mechanical energy because it has both kinetic energy and gravitational potential energy. An object's mechanical energy can be all potential energy, all kinetic energy, or a combination of potential and kinetic energy.

EVIDENCE NOTEBOOK

9. How do the potential energy and kinetic energy of a domino change as it topples over? Record your evidence.

Energy in a Thunderstorm

A thunderstorm displays several forms of energy:

- Lightning is electrical and electromagnetic energy.
- Thunder is sound energy.
- Blowing wind has sound energy and mechanical energy.
- Falling rain has sound energy and mechanical energy.

Thermal Energy Thermal energy is the total kinetic energy of all the particles that make up an object. Particles move faster at higher temperatures than at lower temperatures. The faster the particles in an object move, the more thermal energy the object has. Also, the more particles an object has, the more thermal energy it has.

Electromagnetic Energy Electromagnetic energy is the kinetic energy of electromagnetic waves, which include visible light, x-rays, and microwaves. X-rays are high-energy waves used by doctors and dentists to look at your bones. Microwaves can be used to cook food or to transmit cellphone calls.

Sound Energy Sound energy is kinetic energy caused by the vibration of particles in a medium, such as steel, water, or air. When you pluck the strings of a guitar, they vibrate, producing sound. These vibrations travel outward from the guitar, and transfer energy to air around the strings. As the particles of the air vibrate, they transfer the sound energy to other particles. The vibrating particles do work on special structures in your ear that allow you to interpret the vibrations as sound.

Electrical Energy Electrical energy is the kinetic energy of moving electric charges. The electrical energy that powers a toaster oven or the light bulb in a lamp is caused by negatively charged particles moving in a wire. The more electric charges that are moving, the more electrical energy is carried by the wire. Electrical energy can occur in nature in the form of lightning and smaller static electricity shocks.

Elastic Energy Elastic energy is the potential mechanical energy stored in an object when work is performed to change its shape. You can observe this energy when you stretch a rubber band or squeeze a spring.

Chemical Energy Chemical energy is the potential energy stored in the chemical bonds of substances. The chemical energy in a compound depends on the position and arrangement of the atoms in the compound. Sources of chemical energy include batteries, fuels, and matches. The foods you eat also contain chemical energy.

Nuclear Energy Nuclear energy is the potential energy stored in the nucleus of an atom. When an atom's nucleus breaks apart or when the nuclei of two small atoms join together, energy is released. The energy given off by the sun comes from nuclear energy. The sun's light and heat come from these reactions. Without nuclear energy from the sun, life would not exist on Earth.

Energy Transfer and Energy Transformation

When you roll a ball across a surface, you know that the ball has kinetic energy because it is moving. What will happen if the rolling ball then hits another ball at rest? The ball that is at rest will also start rolling, which means that it now has kinetic energy, as well. This is an example of *energy transfer*. When two objects collide, each exerts a force on the other that can cause energy to pass from one to the other. In this case, kinetic energy is transferred from one ball to the other.

The two balls will also make a noise as they collide, indicating that sound energy has been produced. This is an example of an *energy transformation*, or the change of one form of energy into another. Any form of energy can turn into another form of energy in an energy transformation. Most of the technology you rely on throughout your day depends on energy transfers and transformations. All forms of transportation require energy transformations: riding a bicycle depends on the transformation of chemical energy within your body into mechanical energy from your muscles, which is transferred to the bike pedals and the rest of the bike's gear system. Traveling by car or bus requires the transformation of chemical energy from fuel or a battery into thermal and mechanical energy in order to power its engine, which transfers mechanical energy to the drive chain.

Identify Energy Sources

The electronic devices we rely on every day work by transforming electrical energy into signals that produce electromagnetic, sound, and thermal energy. In portable devices, this electrical energy comes from chemical energy stored in the system's battery. But even this energy must come from somewhere—each time you plug in a tablet or phone to recharge, it converts electrical energy from the electrical grid into the chemical energy stored in the battery. Knowing the source of such energy has become important for people concerned about fossil fuel and renewable energy usage.

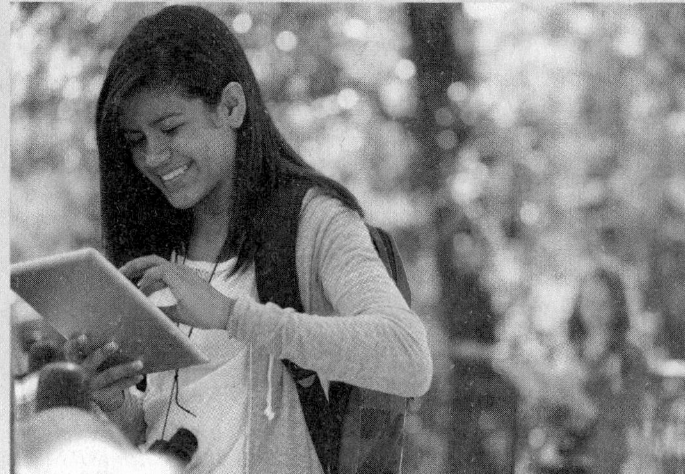

Electronic devices transform electrical energy into electromagnetic, sound, and thermal energy.

10. Think of a technology or appliance you use regularly. Identify the transfers and transformations of energy necessary to operate the technology. What do you think is the original source of the energy?

Observing Energy in Systems

Did you know that the chemical energy in the food you eat originally comes from the sun's energy? Electromagnetic energy from the sun travels to Earth. Plants change this energy into chemical energy through the process of photosynthesis. Animals then eat the plants and change the chemical energy stored in sugars within the plants into other forms of chemical energy within their bodies. Your body also stores the chemical energy from the food you eat (from plants or animals) so it can be used as kinetic mechanical energy when you need it for everything from scratching an itch to running a marathon. This entire process is an example of an energy system.

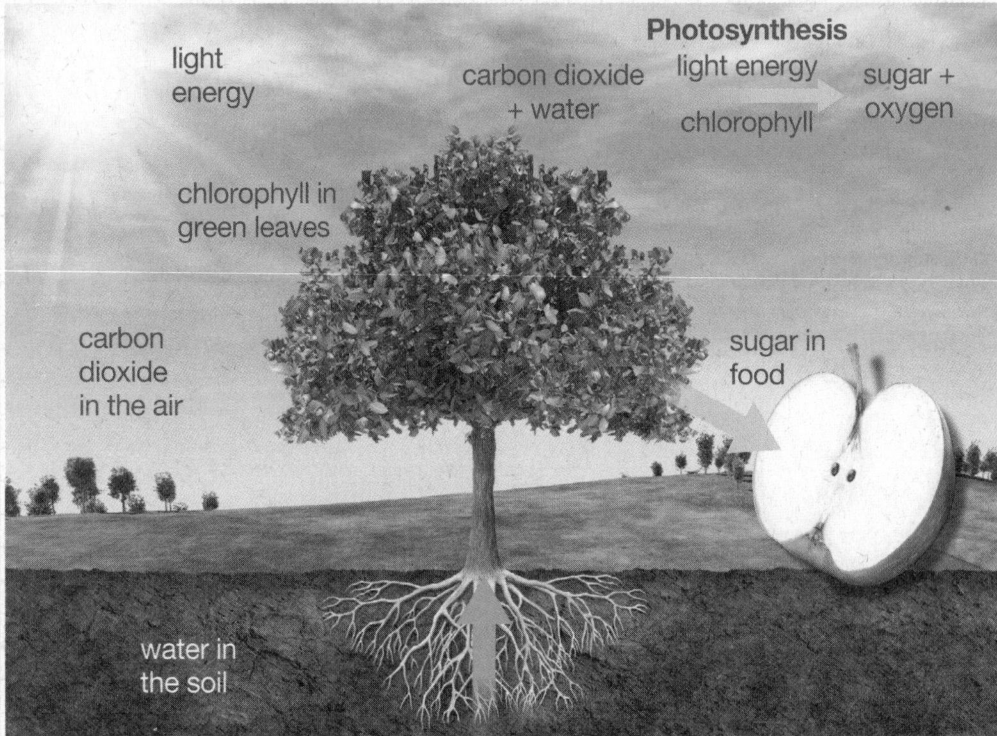

Energy flows through the process of photosynthesis.

11. Consider a tennis racket as a simple system. The racket consists of a metal frame and strings. When a tennis player swings the racket, the player transfers kinetic / potential energy to the racket. As the tennis ball applies a force to the strings on the racket, the strings stretch and for a moment the strings have increased their elastic / chemical energy. The strings rebound and the racket transfers / transforms kinetic energy back to the tennis ball.

Energy in Systems

As you recall, a **system** is a group of interacting parts that move or work together. In order to do work on any one part of a system, energy has to be put into the system. Once it is in the system, energy can then be transferred from one part of the system to another. Energy can also be transformed from one form of energy to another. The system produces results, or outputs, too. Consider a tree as an example of a system. Energy from the sun is one input. One output of this system is the chemical energy in the parts of the tree, which is stored as sugars and other carbohydrates.

Types of Systems

Systems may be natural, such as a tree, or they can be designed, such as a wind-up toy. Systems can also involve a combination of natural and designed parts interacting. A hydroelectric dam is a system that combines the natural system of a river and the designed system of a dam. The natural system consists of the water, the nearby land, and the living things in and around it. The designed system includes the wall that holds back the water as well as the generators and other equipment and structures that transform the mechanical energy of the flowing water into electrical energy.

Hydroelectric Dam System

Flowing water from the river serves as the input to the dam system. Mechanical energy from the flowing water is transferred to the generators. The generators transform mechanical energy to electrical energy, the system's output.

Energy in Designed Systems

As you have already seen, every system that needs energy to operate requires an input of energy from an outside source. This initial energy can then be harnessed through a series of energy transfers and transformations to produce work or another desired outcome. Energy is often expensive, with different drawbacks and benefits associated with each energy source. For this reason, a major focus of scientific and engineering research is finding ways to use energy most effectively. The amount of energy required for a device to work varies greatly, as does the amount of energy available from different sources. The table below shows the estimated amounts of energy in joules associated with a variety of items.

Energy Source	Energy (J)
1 AA battery	1×10^4
1 fully charged smartphone battery	2×10^4
electricity used by a microwave to heat a bowl of soup	2.5×10^5

Energy Source	Energy (J)
1 stick of dynamite	2×10^6
1 gallon of gasoline	1.3×10^8
electricity used by a refrigerator over 1 year	1.5×10^9

12. Do the Math The energy values in the table are shown in scientific notation, which helps to compare very large and very small numbers. The exponents represent the number of times the value is multiplied by 10. For example, 1×10^4 J is equal to 10,000 J. Based on the values in the table, how many smartphone batteries would be required to power a refrigerator for a year?

Hands-On Lab

Investigate Energy in a Rollback Can

You will observe the movements of a device called a rollback can and relate your observations to the energy of the rollback can system.

MATERIALS
- masking tape
- rollback can
- tape measure

Procedure and Analysis

STEP 1 Analyze the rollback can that your teacher provided. Sketch the can and the parts inside it. Identify the parts of the can, and describe how they are connected.

STEP 2 Predict what will happen if you put the can on the floor and push it away from you.

STEP 3 Test your prediction. Use masking tape to mark off a starting line, and push the can from this line. Then use more masking tape to mark the farthest distance the can traveled. Measure that distance with a tape measure. Record your observations.

STEP 4 Describe the energy inputs of this system.

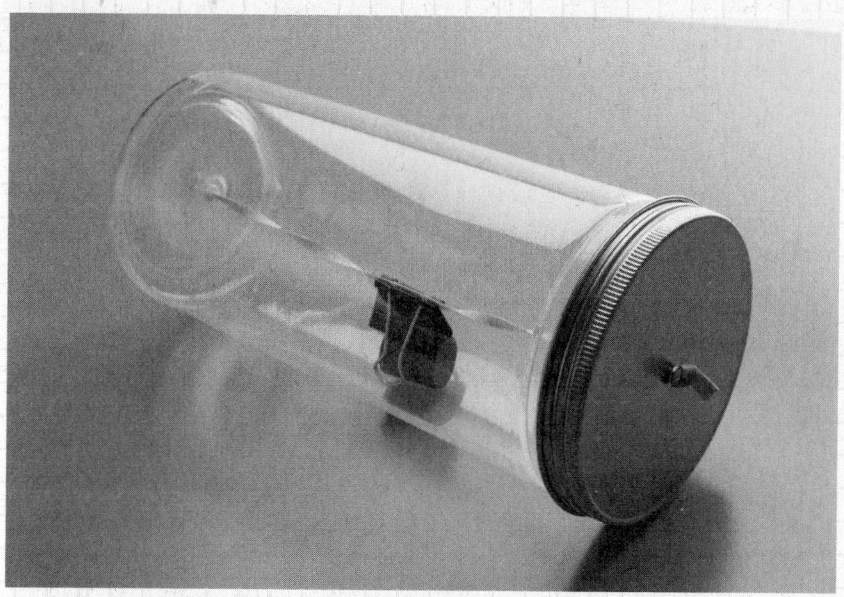

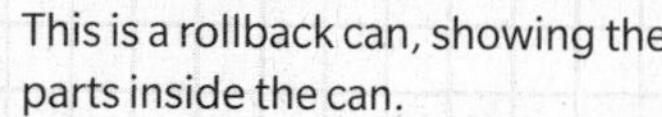
This is a rollback can, showing the parts inside the can.

STEP 5 Why is the device called a "rollback can"? Describe how the movement of the can indicates that the energy of the system is changing.

STEP 6 Consider what is happening inside the can as you push it. What happens to the rubber bands? Describe how energy is stored within the system.

STEP 7 How could you get the can to roll even farther away from you and then return? Explain why you think these changes will give the desired results.

STEP 8 Determine the variables you are testing. Conduct several trials to test your ideas. Record your data, and identify any relationships you observe.

EVIDENCE NOTEBOOK

13. What types of energy transfers and energy transformations are involved in the domino chain reaction? Record your evidence.

Investigate Energy Management

You have seen that kinetic and potential energy can take many forms. A serious concern of engineers and scientists today is energy storage. While the electrical grid can deliver energy to homes and businesses, it cannot save energy for later use. Energy is generally difficult to store efficiently. For this reason, new technologies are constantly under development for storing energy in a variety of ways: as mechanical potential energy in water pump systems, as thermal energy in thermal energy storage systems, or as chemical potential energy in batteries. New advances in chemical battery technology will allow people to generate and store their own energy at home. The energy input for these systems often comes from solar panels installed outside the home.

This wall battery system is installed in a residential garage. It stores electrical energy from a home solar electric system and can be used to power the home or an electric car.

Another issue for energy consumers and producers is energy distribution. The delivery of energy must be carefully controlled—too much or too little energy released at once can be disastrous. The distribution of energy over time is referred to as *power*, or the rate of doing work.

14. You can determine from the table on page 14 that the energy stored in a gallon of gasoline is actually 65 times greater than the energy stored in a stick of dynamite. However, the energy in a stick of dynamite is released all in one instant, while the energy from a gallon of gasoline is usually released in a more controlled manner. Why is the rate at which energy is output from a system important?

Continue Your Exploration

Name: Date:

Check out the path below or go online to choose one of the other paths shown.

Perpetual Motion

- **Hands-On Labs**
- **Ancient Structures**
- **Propose Your Own Path**

Go online to choose one of these other paths.

Throughout history, many clever inventors have tried to engineer machines that, once started, would run forever without any additional energy. Called *perpetual motion machines*, these machines would use as much energy as they generate. Such a machine could theoretically run forever.

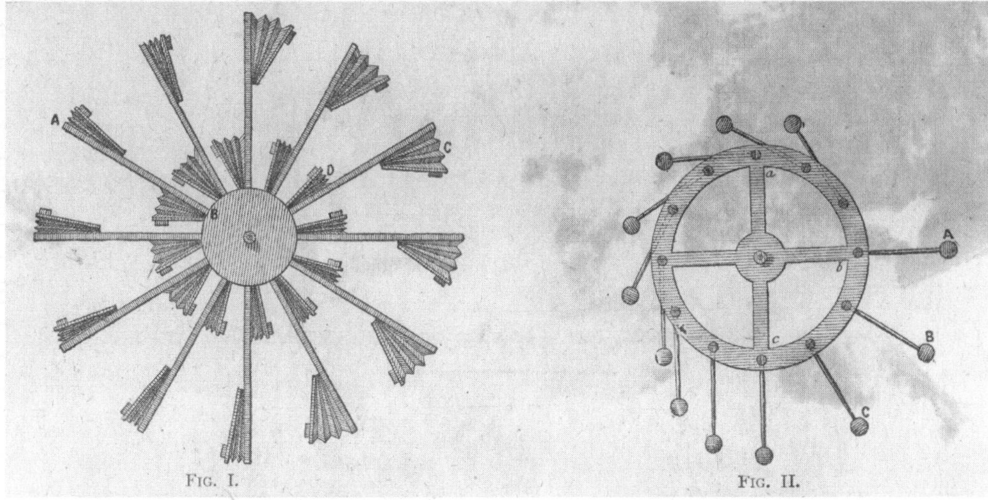

Bernard Launy and Jeremie Metz invented early examples of the overbalanced wheel perpetual motion machine.

The overbalanced wheel perpetual motion machine is one of the most commonly proposed perpetual motion machine designs. The wheel is designed to turn clockwise. Just after a weighted spoke reaches the top of the wheel, the spoke flips outward to the right, exerting a force downward toward the ground. The resulting imbalance in forces on the upward side and downward side of the wheel is expected to keep the wheel turning. The problem is, no matter how smoothly the wheel turns, some energy will be lost from friction as the mechanism rubs on the inner spoke. More energy will also be lost when it is transformed into sound and thermal energy.

1. Analyze the devices invented by Bernard Launy and Jeremie Metz, and identify the flaws in the system in terms of energy inputs and outputs.

Continue Your Exploration

Picture an electric motor and a generator linked so that the generator powers the motor and the motor drives the generator. Once the generator is started, the motor is set into motion. The motion of the motor would then provide the energy to run the generator.

2. Predict whether the motor and generator system would run forever. Explain your reasoning.

3. No one has ever been able to design a successful perpetual motion machine. What condition would have to exist for perpetual motion to be possible?

4. Collaborate Discuss with a partner the usefulness of a perpetual motion machine. If a perpetual motion machine could be built in real life, could it be used to do work?

Can You Explain It?

Name: Date:

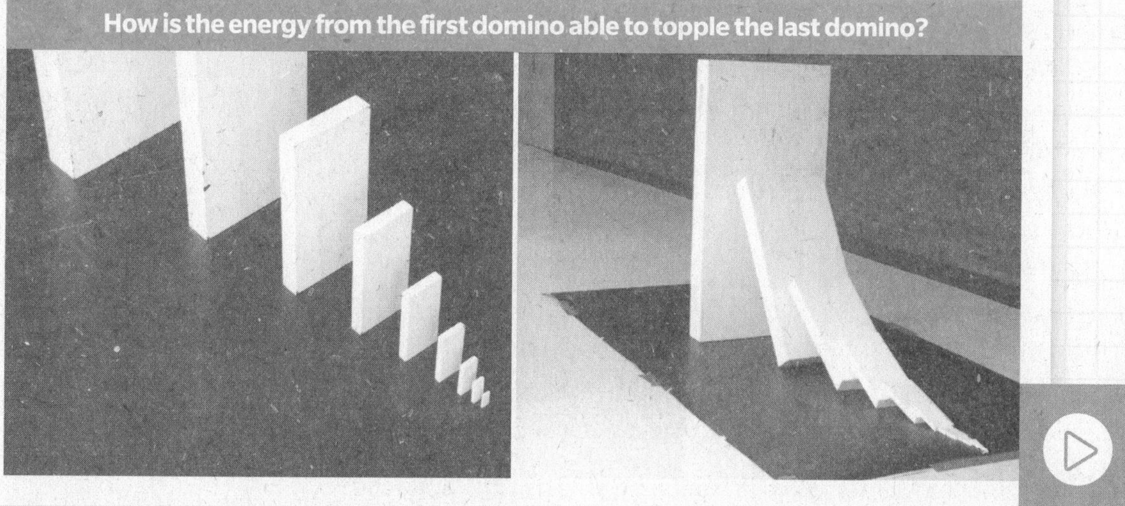
How is the energy from the first domino able to topple the last domino?

Explore ONLINE!

EVIDENCE NOTEBOOK

Refer to the notes in your Evidence Notebook to help you construct an explanation for what happens to the energy within the domino chain reaction system.

1. State your claim. Make sure your claim fully explains what happens to the energy of the first domino when it is toppled.

2. Summarize the evidence you have gathered to support your claim and explain your reasoning.

Checkpoints

Answer the following questions to check your understanding of the lesson.

Use the photo to answer Questions 3–4.

3. As the nail is hammered into the wood, is work being done? How do you know?

A. No, work is not being done. The force from the hammer is being applied to the nail, but the nail moved only a little bit into the wood.

B. No, work is not being done. The nail moved into the wood because of the force from the hammer, but energy was not transferred to the wood.

C. Yes, work is being done. Energy is being transferred from the nail to the hammer, as the nail is driven down into the wood.

D. Yes, work is being done. The force from the hammer is being applied to the nail, and the nail is moving a distance into the wood.

4. What forms of energy are involved in hammering the nail into the wood? Choose all that apply.

A. sound energy

B. electrical energy

C. kinetic energy

D. electromagnetic energy

Use the photo to answer Question 5.

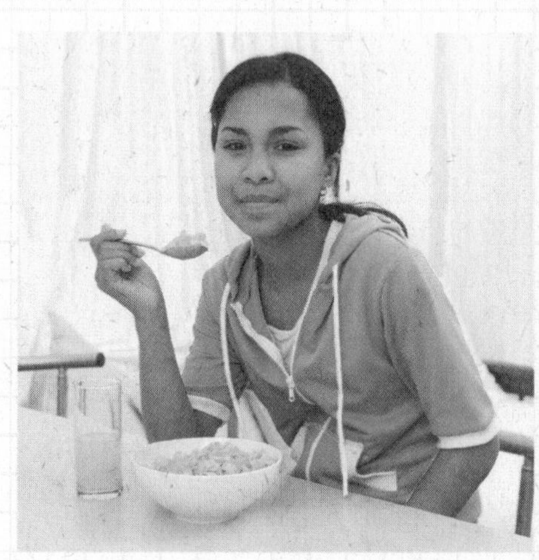

5. Eating a healthy breakfast gives your body the energy needed to help you start your day. The girl in the photo is having cereal and orange juice, which have stored thermal / chemical energy, a form of kinetic / potential energy. The girl's body breaks down the components of the food to access the energy stored in them. Later in the day, some of this energy is transformed into the kinetic / potential energy that will allow the girl to study and play sports. Some of the energy is also transformed into thermal / sound energy that keeps her body warm.

---

6. The energy in a flashlight is provided by the electromagnetic / chemical energy from the batteries. This energy is transformed into electrical / sound energy, which travels along a wire to a light bulb. There, it is transformed into electromagnetic energy. This energy is one of the inputs / outputs. The other is chemical / thermal energy that you can feel as flashlight gets warmer.

Interactive Review

Complete this section to review the main concepts of the lesson.

Energy is the ability to do work or cause changes in matter. There are many forms of energy in everyday life, and each is a form of potential or kinetic energy.

A. Give two examples of a person doing different amounts of work on an object. Use the formula for work to explain how you know the amount of work in each example is different.

A system is a group of interacting parts that move or work together. Energy is transferred and transformed as it moves between components within a system.

B. Describe a simple system where energy is transferred to the system, transformed at least once, and then energy is transferred out of the system. Describe the types and forms of energy in the system.

Kinetic and Potential Energy

This skier has a mix of kinetic and potential energy.

By the end of this lesson . . .

you will be able to analyze a system's kinetic and potential energy.

Go online to view the digital version of the Hands-On Lab for this lesson and to download additional lab resources.

CAN YOU EXPLAIN IT?

Why doesn't the water balloon hit the student's face?

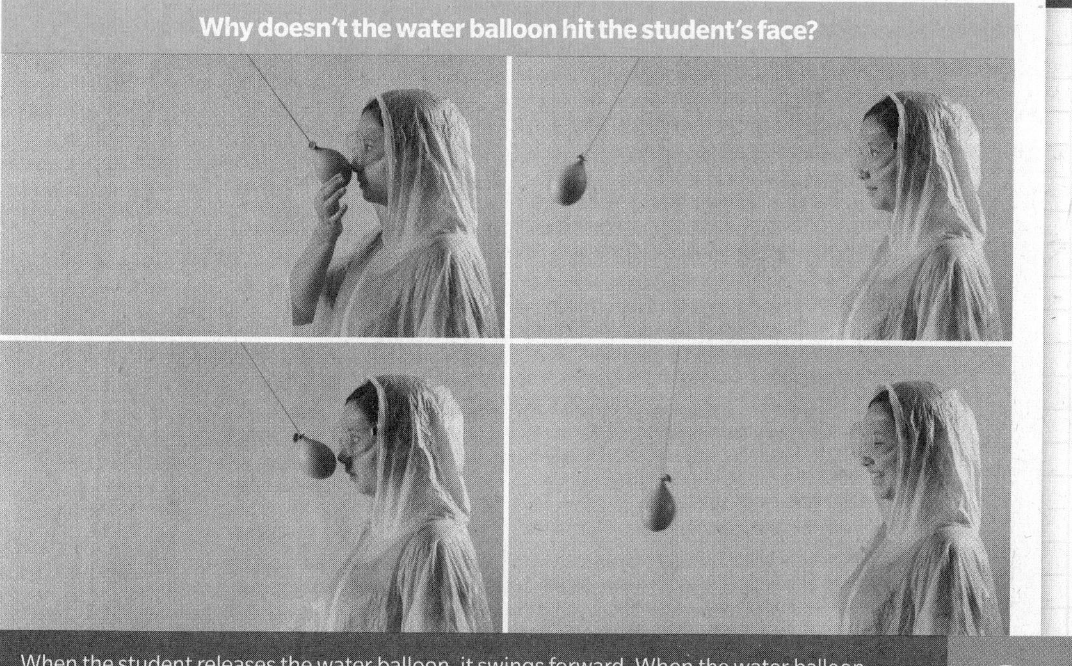

When the student releases the water balloon, it swings forward. When the water balloon swings back, you can tell that the student expects the water balloon to hit her face. Why does the water balloon not continue on and hit the student's face?

1. Based on what you know about energy, what types of energy does the water balloon have? How could energy explain the water balloon's behavior?

EVIDENCE NOTEBOOK As you explore the lesson, gather evidence to help explain how energy affects the motion of the water balloon.

Explaining Kinetic and Potential Energy

Every object has energy associated with it. That energy can be due to the position of the object, the object's motion, the chemical bonds that make up the object, or many other factors. Identifying the types and forms of energy that an object has can help you model the behavior of the object.

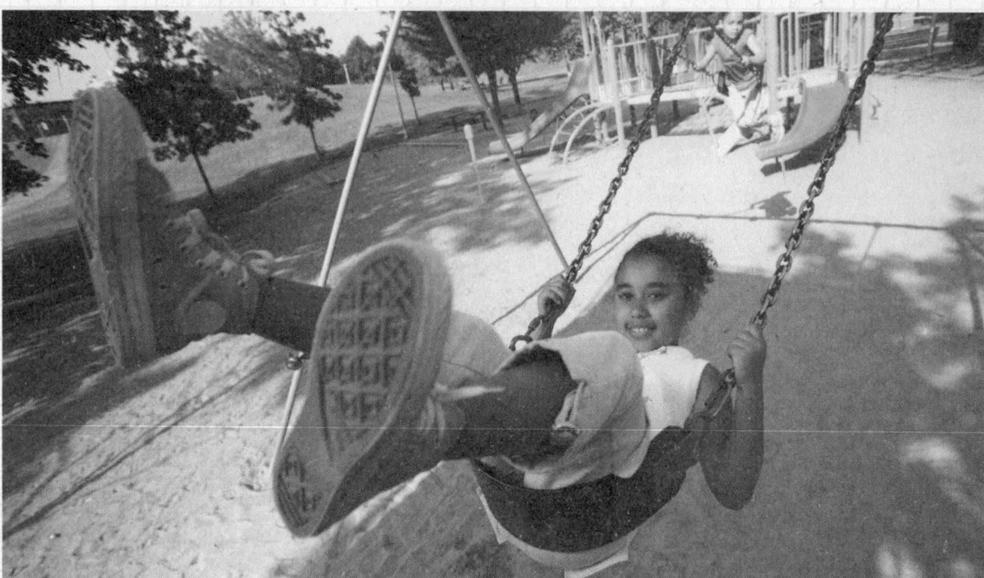

Energy is present in every situation. The two students swinging both have energy, but there is also energy in everything else in the photo.

2. What are some types and forms of energy that might be present in this photo?

3. Which statement best describes a type or form of energy present in this photo?

A. There is potential energy in the movement of the arrow.

B. There is kinetic energy in the movement of the arrow.

C. There is kinetic energy due to the arrow's position above the ground.

After an arrow is shot from a bow, it will fly through the air.

Kinetic Energy

Whenever an object is moving, it has the ability to do work. For instance, imagine a baseball bat being swung through the air. If a bat hits a ball, the ball will move.

The swinging bat has the ability to apply a force on another object and move that object in the direction of the force. This is known as doing work on the object. Because every moving object has the ability to do work, every moving object has kinetic energy. Kinetic energy is the energy associated with motion.

4. This archer has pulled back the string and flexed the bow in order to launch an arrow. The flexed bow has potential / kinetic energy. The energy in the bow is due to its motion / condition. When the string is released, work will be done on the bow / arrow.

Potential Energy

An object does not need to be moving to have the ability to do work. Imagine a stretched rubber band. You could shoot that rubber band across the room or release it to move another object. The rubber band has the ability to do work because it has been stretched, not because it is moving. Potential energy is the energy an object has because of its position, condition, or chemical composition. The stretched condition of the rubber band gives it the ability to do work when it is released and its potential energy is transformed to kinetic energy. Likewise, imagine placing a ball at the top of a ramp. Because of the ball's position, it now has the potential to do work when it is released and its potential energy is transformed to kinetic energy.

5. Which of the following forms of potential energy do you think this cat has?

   A. elastic potential energy

   B. magnetic potential energy

   C. electrical potential energy

   D. gravitational potential energy

This cat is standing off the ground, on a cat toy.

Forms of Potential Energy

Some forms of potential energy depend on an object's condition. *Elastic potential energy* is the energy associated with objects that are stretched or compressed. A rubber band has elastic potential energy when it is stretched. Because a rubber band will move to return to its unstretched shape, it has the ability to do work. Other forms of potential energy depend on the chemical composition of an object. Food gives us energy because it has *chemical potential energy* stored in the bonds between atoms.

Gravitational, electrical, and magnetic potential energy all depend on the positions of objects. Gravity, electricity, and magnetism generate forces at a distance. Objects fall to Earth. Iron is attracted to magnets. Your hair is attracted to a charged balloon. Anything acted on by one of these forces has potential energy due to its position. For example, if a magnetic force moves a piece of iron, work is done. The force on the iron and the distance that the iron can move depend on how close it is to a magnet. Since work is a force applied over a distance, the potential for work depends on the iron's position. Therefore, the potential energy of the iron depends on its position.

Gravitational Potential Energy

Gravitational potential energy is the energy an object has due to its position relative to Earth. In everyday life, this means how high above the ground an object is. A pencil that falls off of a table will fall toward the ground. Due to its height and to gravity, the pencil has the potential to do work. If you drop the pencil from near the ceiling, the pencil will have more time to accelerate. It will travel farther and hit the ground with more force. Because the pencil was higher, it had more potential to do work. Gravitational potential energy has a special importance because it constantly affects every object in the universe. We see the effects of gravitational potential energy every day.

Identify Types of Energy

6. **Draw** Choose a group of objects that you can see from where you are working. Draw a diagram of the objects. Label the objects that have kinetic or gravitational potential energy in your drawing.

Analyzing Kinetic and Potential Energy

The energy of an object depends on many factors. Different types and forms of energy are affected by different factors. For instance, kinetic energy depends on the mass and speed of an object. Gravitational potential energy depends on the mass of an object, but also on its height above the ground.

This student riding a bike has kinetic energy.

This moving car also has kinetic energy.

7. Which of these objects do you think has more kinetic energy? Explain your answer.

8. Which object would be able to do more work? Explain your answer.

Mass, Speed, and Kinetic Energy

The kinetic energy of an object depends on both the mass and the speed of the object. Kinetic energy is the energy due to motion. An object that is moving more quickly will have more kinetic energy than an identical object moving more slowly. For instance, imagine that you ask your friend to lend you a pen. If your friend gently tosses the pen to you, it will have much less energy than if your friend throws the pen with a lot of force. The faster the pen is moving, the more kinetic energy it will have.

Increasing an object's mass will also increase its kinetic energy. Imagine a table tennis ball and a golf ball. The two balls are about the same size. However, if they were thrown at the same speed, the golf ball would be able to do more work because it has more mass.

Do the Math | Graph Kinetic Energy

9. Make a graph using the data in the table. The table shows the kinetic energy of several different balls moving at the same speed. Graph the mass of the balls on the x-axis and the kinetic energy of the balls on the y-axis.

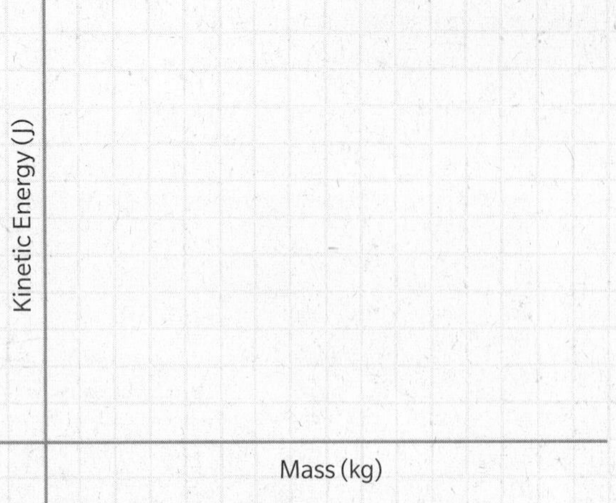

Mass (kg)	Kinetic Energy (J)
1.0	2
2.5	5
3.0	6
5.0	10

10. Circle the graph that your plotted points most resemble to identify the relationship between mass and kinetic energy.

A. $y = x$

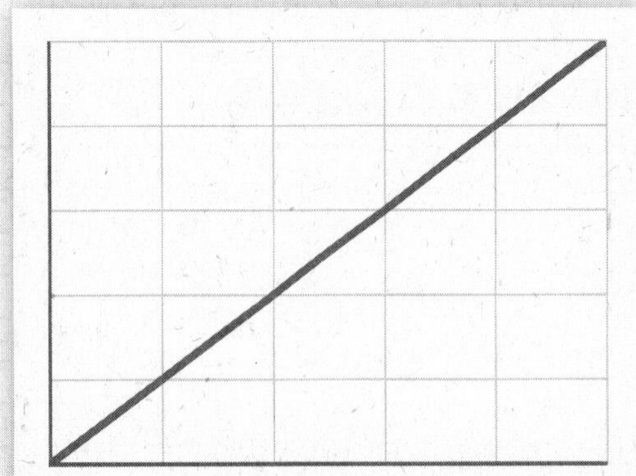

B. $y = x^2$

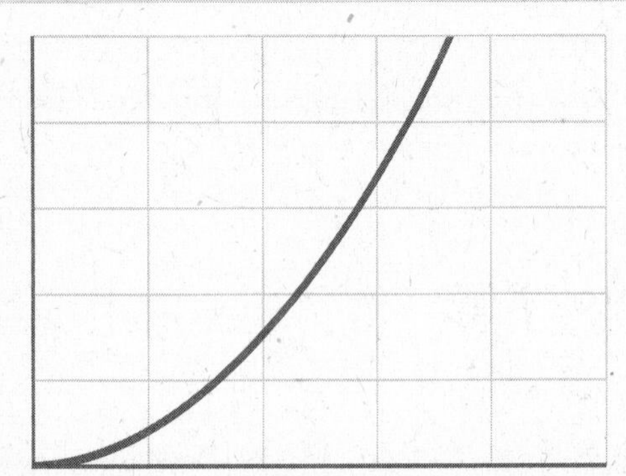

11. Make a graph using the data in the table. The table shows the kinetic energy of one ball moving at various speeds. The same ball was used in every roll, so the mass is constant. Graph the speed of the ball on the x-axis and the kinetic energy of the ball on the y-axis.

Kinetic Energy (J)

Speed (m/s)

Speed (m/s)	Kinetic Energy (J)
1	1
3	9
4	16
6	36

12. Circle the graph that your plotted points most resemble to identify the relationship between speed and kinetic energy.

A. $y = x$

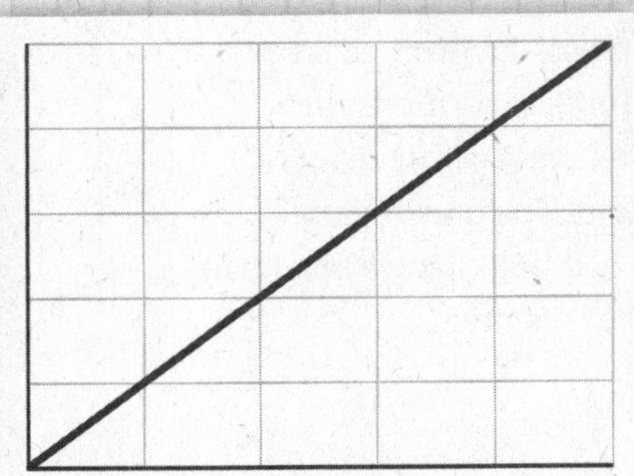

B. $y = x^2$

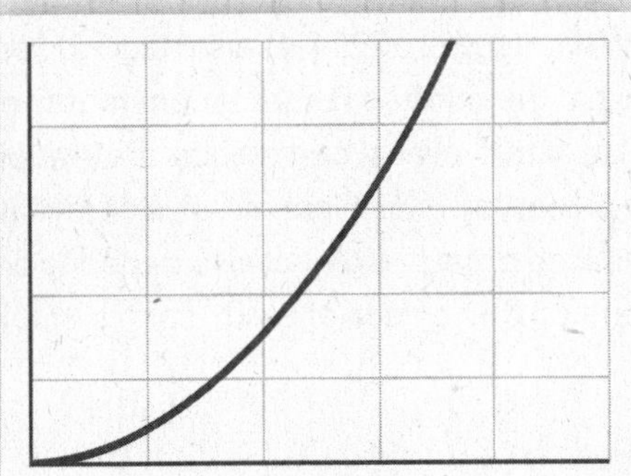

13. Describe the relationship between kinetic energy and mass, and give an example of how changing an object's mass changes its kinetic energy. Also describe the relationship between kinetic energy and speed, and give an example of how changing an object's speed would affect its kinetic energy.

The Equation for Kinetic Energy

The kinetic energy of an object depends on both the mass and the speed of the moving object. However, as you have identified, increasing the speed of the object will increase the kinetic energy a lot more than increasing the mass of the object. The equation that we use to find the kinetic energy of an object is:

$$\textbf{kinetic energy} = \frac{1}{2}mv^2$$

In this equation, m represents the mass of the object and v represents the speed of the object. Remember that v^2 is the same as $v \times v$. If there were a 2 kg ball moving at 3 m/s, you would calculate the kinetic energy like this:

$$\textbf{kinetic energy} = \frac{1}{2}mv^2$$

$$\textbf{kinetic energy} = \frac{1}{2} \times (2\ \text{kg}) \times (3\ \text{m/s})^2$$

$$\textbf{kinetic energy} = \frac{1}{2} \times (2\ \text{kg}) \times (3\ \text{m/s}) \times (3\ \text{m/s})$$

$$\textbf{kinetic energy} = 9\ \text{kg} \cdot \text{m}^2/\text{s}^2 = 9\ \text{J}$$

Gravitational Potential Energy

The gravitational potential energy of an object depends on the object's height. The farther an object can fall, the more gravitational potential energy it has. The gravitational potential energy of an object also depends on the object's mass. If two objects are moving at the same speed, the more massive object will be able to do more work. Because of this, even when objects are stationary, a massive object will have more potential energy than a less massive object at the same height. The gravitational potential energy of an object also depends on the strength of gravity. However, gravity is constant on the surface of Earth, so this is not a factor most of the time.

Language SmArts
Argue Using Evidence

Potential Energy vs Height

This graph shows the relationship between the height of an object and the object's gravitational potential energy.

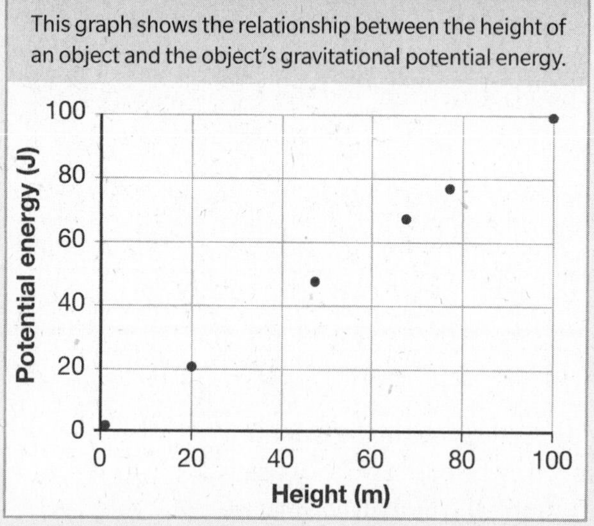

Potential Energy vs Mass

This graph shows the relationship between the mass of an object and the object's gravitational potential energy.

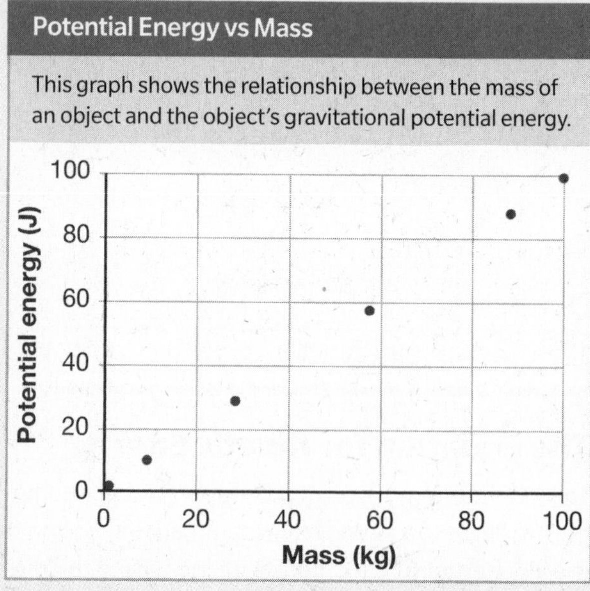

14. Look at the graphs of gravitational potential energy, height, and mass. Based on these graphs, does either height or mass affect the gravitational potential energy more, or do these two factors seem to have similar effects?

The Equation for Gravitational Potential Energy

As you have seen, the gravitational potential energy of an object depends on the mass of the object and the height of the object. However, unlike the factors that affect kinetic energy, both factors affect the potential energy to the same degree.

gravitational potential energy = *mgh*

In this equation, *m* represents the mass of the object and *g* represents the acceleration due to gravity. On Earth, $g = 9.8\ m/s^2$. Finally, *h* represents the height of the object. If there were a 10 kg rock held 1 m above the surface of Earth, you could solve for the rock's gravitational potential energy like this:

gravitational potential energy = *mgh*

gravitational potential energy = $(10\ kg) \times (9.8\ m/s^2) \times (1\ m)$

gravitational potential energy = $98\ kg \cdot m^2/s^2 = 98\ J$

EVIDENCE NOTEBOOK

15. How does the gravitational potential energy of the water balloon before it was released compare with the gravitational potential energy of the water balloon when it returns almost to its release position? Record your evidence.

Engineer It

Measure Potential Energy

Unlike an object with kinetic energy, an object with only potential energy is not moving. A stretched spring is not in motion, and neither is a box sitting on a shelf. With a moving object, you can test how much work the object can do. You can hit a baseball with a bat or see how far a box that you push will move before friction stops it. Measuring the potential energy of an object can be trickier.

16. How could you measure the amount of elastic potential energy in a stretched rubber band? Think about the definition of energy when planning your investigation.

(100Kg) x 9.8m/s² x 2m)

980 Kg·m²/s² =

PE = 100 x 2 x 9.8

Analyzing Energy in Systems

Kinetic and Potential Energy of Objects

As we have seen, the energy in an object or system of objects may be either kinetic or potential energy, or both. For instance, a falling ball will have both kinetic and gravitational potential energy. The kinetic energy comes from the ball's motion through the air. The ball is moving, so it has kinetic energy. The ball also has mass and is above the ground, so it must also have gravitational potential energy. Even though the ball is currently falling, it has the potential to fall even farther and accelerate more. Thus, the ball has a mix of both kinetic and potential energy.

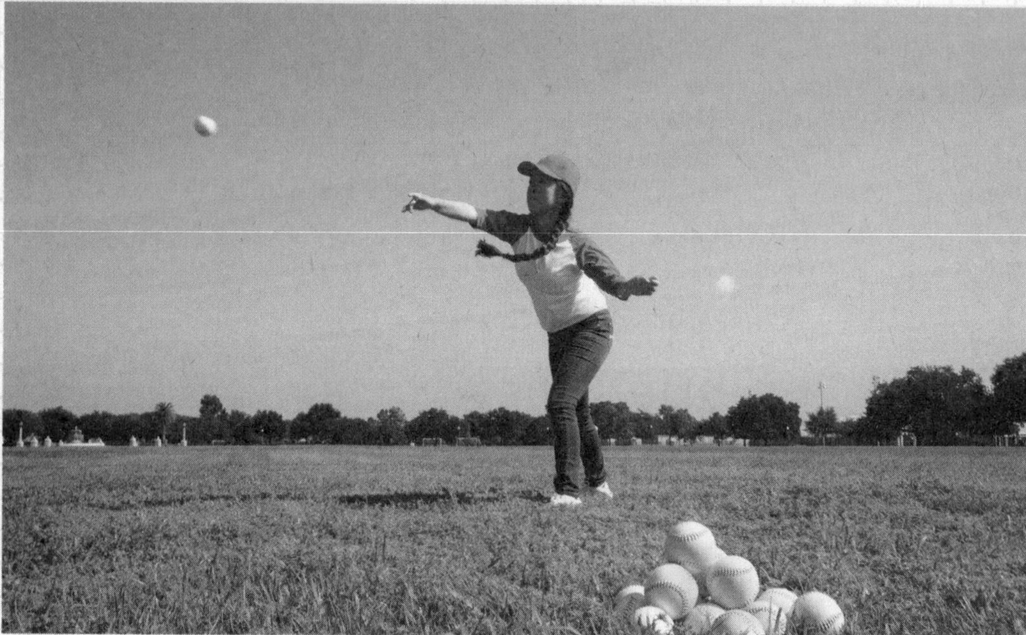

As it flies through the air, the baseball is moving and it is also above the ground.

17. Compare the energy of the ball in the air with the energy of one of the balls on the ground. Explain why the amount, type, and form of the energy might be different or the same.

Kinetic and Potential Energy in Systems

Energy is not created or destroyed but it is transferred between objects and it can be transformed into different types and forms of energy. Because of this, systems are useful for examining energy. We can model how energy moves through a system. We can also use the systems view to track how energy is being added to a system as an input and how energy is being lost from a system as an output.

Roller Coaster

The cars of a roller coaster often have a mix of kinetic and potential energy. The amount of each type of energy changes as the cars go up and down.

18. The roller coaster cars move very slowly at the top of the hill, so they have little kinetic energy. The speed of the cars increases as they move down the hill; this increases the cars' kinetic energy. Where might this extra kinetic energy have come from?

A. kinetic energy was transformed into potential energy

B. the cars always had kinetic energy

C. potential energy was transformed into kinetic energy

D. kinetic energy was added by pushing the cars

Energy Transformations

Energy can be transformed from one type to another. For instance, if you were to hold a ball above your head, it would have gravitational potential energy. When you dropped the ball, it would begin to fall. The farther the ball falls, the less gravitational potential energy it has. However, when the ball is falling, it is also moving and has kinetic energy. The longer the ball falls, the faster it will move as it accelerates toward Earth. As its speed increases, so will its kinetic energy. The gravitational potential energy is being transformed into kinetic energy.

Energy in a Mechanical System

As the roller coaster cars go up the hill, their kinetic energy is transformed into potential energy. At the top of the hill, the cars are barely moving and have a large amount of potential energy. As the cars go down the hill, their potential energy is transformed into kinetic energy. At the bottom of the hill, the cars are moving very quickly and have little gravitational potential energy because of how close they are to the ground. At that point, they have a large amount of kinetic energy.

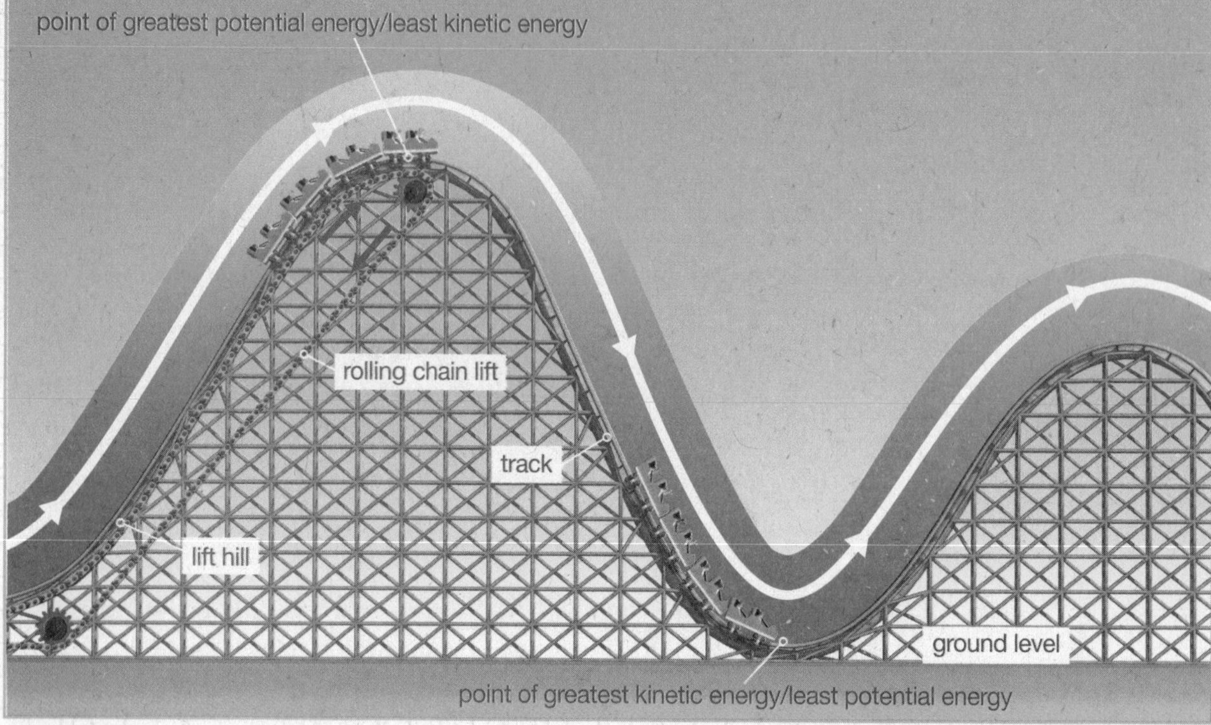

19. Discuss The roller coaster cars in the diagram have no motor in them. The cars are not propelled by anything except their energy. After these cars went down the roller coaster's initial hill, would they be able to go up a taller hill? Explain your answer.

Conservation of Energy

Like matter, energy is conserved. It is not created or destroyed. For this reason, we can track how energy moves through a system. Roller coaster cars can be treated as a system. The cars are lifted up a hill, which gives the system an input of energy. This energy then transforms from potential energy to kinetic energy and back again as the cars go down and up hills on the track. Because no more energy is added to the system during the ride, we know that the cars will never be able to go higher than the peak of the first hill. Not only can the cars go no higher, but some energy is lost due to friction, so the height of hill that the cars can reach decreases throughout the ride. It is important to note, that even though the energy leaves the system of cars, the energy has not disappeared. The energy has been transferred to objects or systems outside of the system of cars.

EVIDENCE NOTEBOOK

20. How does the conservation of energy in a system relate to the water balloon's movement? Record your evidence.

Hands-On Lab

Analyze Energy in Systems

You will evaluate different systems to identify how the kinetic energy and gravitational potential energy of objects change over time. You will treat each situation as a system and analyze how energy moves through the system.

MATERIALS

- ball, bouncy
- ball, large
- hanging mass set
- lab stand
- masking tape
- meterstick
- string

Procedure and Analysis

STEP 1 Use your materials to set up the system described in the first box of the data table.

STEP 2 Observe the system several times. In the table, describe how the kinetic and gravitational potential energy of the object or objects in the system change over time.

STEP 3 Plan out two additional systems using your materials, and record them in the table. Ask your teacher to approve your ideas before moving on.

STEP 4 Repeat Steps 1 and 2 for the two new situations that you have planned out.

System	Observations
A mass hanging from a string, swinging back and forth.	

Analysis

STEP 5 Choose one of the situations that you observed. List any energy inputs or outputs of that system. Consider the different types of energy, and describe the energy transformations that took place in that system.

STEP 6 When does the system you observed have the greatest amount of potential energy?

STEP 7 When does the system you observed have the greatest amount of kinetic energy?

Imagine Energy in a System

21. Write Imagine that you are the energy associated with an object. Pick a mechanical system, such as a bike being pedaled down the mountainside or a bowling ball rolling down the lane toward the pins. Describe how you are changing from one type of energy to another as the object moves and how you are gaining or losing energy through inputs or outputs of the system.

Continue Your Exploration

Name: **Date:**

Check out the path below or go online to choose one of the other paths shown.

Traffic Safety and Energy

- **Hands-On Labs**
- **Energy of a Yo-Yo**
- **Propose Your Own Path**

Go online to choose one of these other paths.

Coasting downhill on a bicycle or swinging as high as possible on a swing can give you a real sense of the energy of motion. If you're like most people, though, you experience the highest levels of kinetic energy when traveling in a car, truck, or bus. Speed limits, highway construction, and safety features on cars and trucks are all influenced by the need to keep people safe when traveling in large vehicles at high speeds.

Automotive safety engineers use computer simulations and crash tests to design and test safety features for all types of vehicles. The larger and faster a vehicle is, the more kinetic energy it has and the more work—or damage—it can do. In an accident, large amounts of energy can be transferred, which can cause a lot of damage. Vehicles are designed to protect people's bodies from the rapid energy transfers and transformations that can occur when large amounts of kinetic energy are involved.

1. What are some factors that affect how much kinetic energy a moving vehicle has? How does the kinetic energy of a car or truck compare to that of a bicycle or motorcycle?

Crash test dummies are used to test how the energy transfers in automobile accidents affect passengers.

Continue Your Exploration

Safety engineers perform crash tests in laboratory environments under specific, controlled conditions. Out on the road, drivers face a much wider variety of situations. Vehicle safety features protect people from the large changes in energy that occur during accidents and sudden stops. Traffic laws are in place to try to prevent such situations from happening in the first place. You have probably noticed that the speed limit on city streets is different from the speed limit on large highways. In some cases, speed limits also change depending on the time of day and are lower near parks, schools, or other facilities.

2. Some states have different speed limits for cars and large trucks. Do you think this is a good idea? Use what you know about kinetic energy to argue for or against this policy.

3. Cars are designed with safety equipment such as crumple zones and air bags. In a collision, parts of the car surrounding the passengers crumple and deform, and air bags inflate. Describe the energy transfers and transformations that occur and how these safety features help keep people safe.

4. Collaborate With a partner, research the masses of cars, trucks, and buses that drive on local streets. Choose an example of each type of vehicle and record the mass for your chosen model. Then research the speed limits in your area for neighborhood streets, city streets, and highways. Based on your research, develop three recommendations that could make traffic safer. What are some questions you have about how kinetic energy is involved in traffic safety laws and policies?

Can You Explain It?

Name: **Date:**

Why doesn't the water balloon hit the student's face?

Explore
ONLINE!

EVIDENCE NOTEBOOK

Refer to the notes in your Evidence Notebook to help you construct an explanation for why the swinging water balloon does not hit the student's face.

1. State your claim. Make sure your claim fully explains why the water balloon does not hit the student's face.

2. Summarize the evidence you have gathered to support your claim, and explain your reasoning.

Checkpoints

Answer the following questions to check your understanding of the lesson.

Use the photo to answer Questions 3 and 4.

3. Suppose the skater is at the highest point in the jump. What are the relative amounts of the skater's kinetic and gravitational potential energy at that point?
   - **A.** all kinetic energy, no gravitational potential energy
   - **B.** half kinetic energy, half gravitational potential energy
   - **C.** no kinetic energy, all gravitational potential energy
   - **D.** no kinetic energy, no gravitational potential energy

4. Which of the following statements about the kinetic and potential energy of the skater are true? You may select more than one answer.
   - **A.** As the skater rolls up the side of the half-pipe, the skater gains kinetic energy.
   - **B.** The skater has no gravitational potential energy at the bottom of the half-pipe.
   - **C.** Gravitational potential energy becomes kinetic energy when the skater rolls down the side of the half-pipe.
   - **D.** The skater transfers gravitational potential energy to the skateboard.

The table describes several objects sitting on a display shelf. Use the table to answer Question 5.

Object	Height (m)	Mass (kg)
Trophy	1.0	4.5
Bowling ball	1.4	7.3
Book	0.5	0.3
Diploma	1.2	0.1

5. Which of the objects in the table has the most gravitational potential energy?
   - **A.** trophy
   - **B.** bowling ball
   - **C.** book
   - **D.** diploma

---

6. Two cars are driving down the road. Car A has a mass of 1100 kg and is moving at 20 m/s. Car B is has a mass of 1000 kg and is moving at 30 m/s. Which car has more kinetic energy and why?
   - **A.** car A because it has more mass and almost the same speed as car B
   - **B.** car B because it has a greater speed and almost the same mass as car A
   - **C.** car A because it has a lower speed and almost the same mass as car B
   - **D.** car B because it has less mass and almost the same speed as car A

Interactive Review

Complete this section to review the main concepts of the lesson.

Kinetic energy is the energy associated with motion. Potential energy is the energy associated with the position, condition, or chemical composition of an object.

A. Choose an object that you can see. Describe its kinetic and potential energy.

Kinetic energy depends on the mass and speed of an object. Speed has a much greater effect on kinetic energy than mass. Gravitational potential energy depends on the mass and height of an object.

B. Explain how changing the speed of an object will affect its kinetic energy.

Kinetic and potential energy changes can be modeled by analyzing how energy moves through a system.

C. Explain how the concepts of energy transformation and conservation of energy allow you to track how energy moves through a system.

Transforming Potential Energy

As riders zoom down the towering hill of the roller coaster, their potential energy transforms into kinetic energy.

By the end of this lesson . . .

you will be able to model and describe how the relative positions of objects in a system change the amount of potential energy in the system.

Go online to view the digital version of the Hands-On Lab for this lesson and to download additional lab resources.

CAN YOU EXPLAIN IT?

Why do these two balls bounce differently?

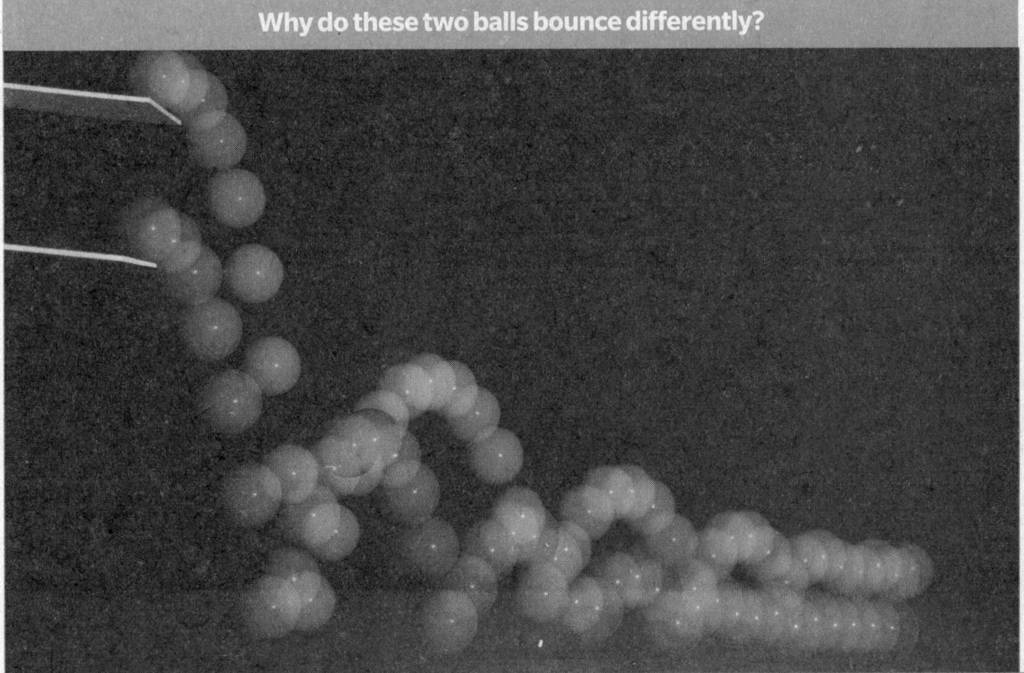

This time-lapse photo shows the paths of two bouncing balls. Other than color, the balls are identical. The two balls begin at rest at different heights. Then they fall to the ground. Notice that the balls do not bounce in quite the same way.

Explore ONLINE!

1. What is the difference between energy transformation and energy transfer?

2. What type of energy does each ball have before it falls? Explain your answer.

EVIDENCE NOTEBOOK As you explore the lesson, gather evidence to help explain why the balls bounce differently.

Analyzing Potential Energy

You may recall that potential energy is the energy an object has because of its position, condition, or chemical composition. It is stored energy, and it can be transformed into kinetic energy to do work. People store energy in many different ways to use for a variety of tasks. Tasks such as riding in a car or bus to get to school meet needs. But some tasks are only for entertainment, such as playing with a pogo stick.

As people jump on pogo sticks, energy is transformed between kinetic and potential energy.

3. The spring in a pogo stick stores energy in the system. Match each description of the spring in the pogo stick system with the state of energy in the system.

spring expands and applies force	minimum elastic potential energy
spring reaches maximum expansion	maximum elastic potential energy
spring is compressed by force	energy enters the system
spring reaches maximum compression	energy leaves the system

Energy in a System

We define the boundaries of a system to help us analyze a situation. Energy can enter or leave a system across its boundaries. This energy transfer is often done by applying a force on the system boundary. In the pogo stick example, the weight of the person on the pogo stick forces the spring of the pogo stick to compress. The person transfers energy to the pogo stick system. When the spring is compressed, it stores this energy as elastic potential energy. When the spring expands, it applies a force back on the person, causing the person to bounce upward. This transfers energy from the pogo stick system back to the person. While the spring is expanding or compressing, the system also has kinetic energy. Energy transforms from potential to kinetic energy and back.

Energy Transfers and Transformations

If work is done on a system or by a system, the amount and the types or forms of energy in the system may change. Adding energy to a system or removing energy from a system may be considered a transfer of energy. When energy stays within a system but changes into a different form, this is called energy transformation. Sometimes a small amount of energy may be added to a system to cause the potential energy of the system to transform into kinetic energy. Imagine a glass sitting on a table. The glass has gravitational potential energy. This potential energy will not transform into kinetic energy unless something happens, such as a person bumping the glass. The force on the glass is now unbalanced. When the bump transfers a small amount of energy to the glass, it does work on the glass. This energy now transforms into kinetic energy as the glass moves or falls.

4. Look at the ramp system in the photo. What is preventing the potential energy in this system from being transformed into kinetic energy?

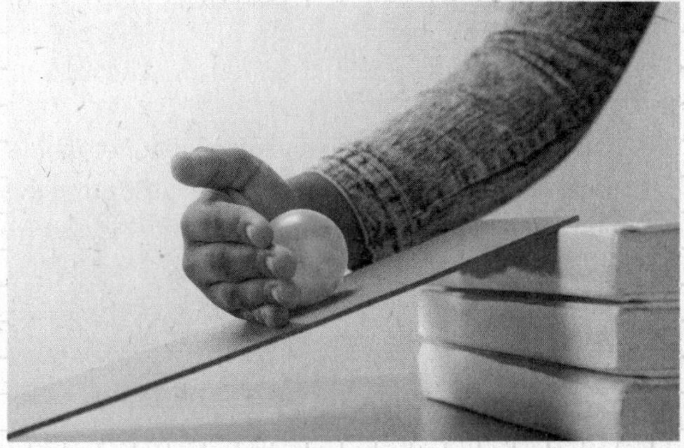

Fields and Potential Energy

A **field** is any region in which a noncontact force has an effect. Objects in a field may be acted upon by a force, depending on the type of field and the type of object. Magnets and magnetic objects in a magnetic field will be acted on by a magnetic force. Similarly, a mass in a gravitational field will be acted on by a gravitational force. Each object will have a different amount of potential energy, depending on its position in the field. The forces in the field will cause the object to move from a position of higher potential energy to a position of lower potential energy, unless another force prevents the object from moving.

Since the force of gravity is an attractive force, you have to apply force to masses to separate them. You are doing work on the masses, which transfers energy to the masses. If the masses are held in these same relative positions, the energy is stored as gravitational potential energy. When you release the masses, gravity pulls them together, transforming the potential energy into kinetic energy as they move together. The potential energy of the system of masses decreases as they move closer to each other. Because the magnetic force between two magnets may be either repulsive or attractive, the change in potential energy of a magnetic system may vary differently.

Potential Energy and Magnetic Fields

5. On the right, redraw the magnet system shown on the left in such a way that the new system has more potential energy than what is currently shown.

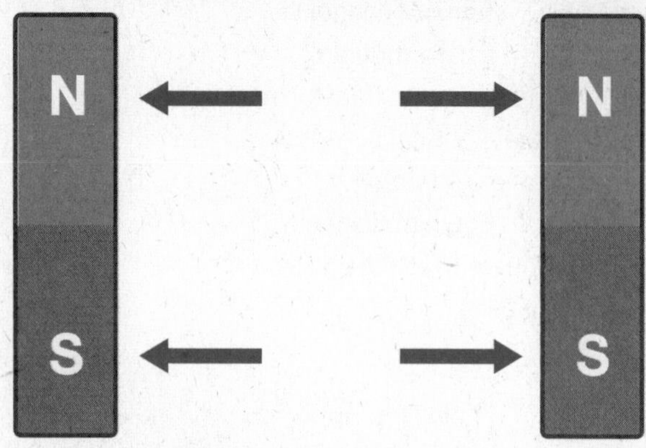

6. Discuss Imagine flipping one of the magnets above so they are attracted to each other. As these magnets are separated, the attractive force decreases, but the potential energy of the system increases. Discuss with a partner how this is possible.

Play with Potential Energy

Many toys and fun activities such as amusement park rides rely on the transformation of potential energy. It is transformed into the energy of motion, sound, and light in ways that are entertaining.

Gravitational Potential Energy

Dominoes, roller coasters, water slides, and many other games transform gravitational potential energy in entertaining ways.

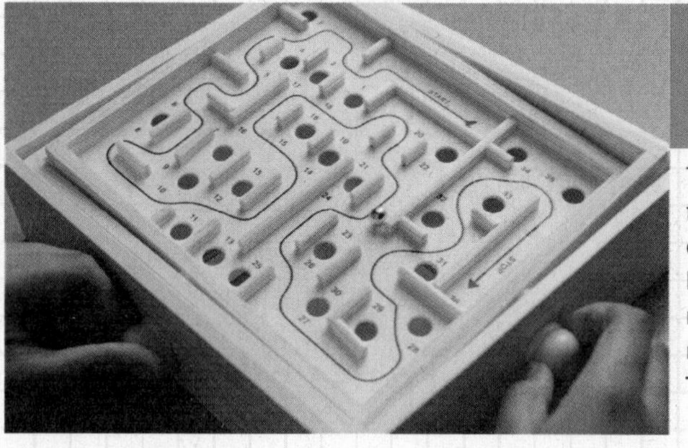

To play a labyrinth game, the player turns the knobs on the outside of the frame to direct the ball around the maze without letting it fall into a hole. One knob tips the maze side to side. The other knob tips the maze forward and back.

7. Think of the labyrinth game in the photo as a system. How is energy transferred into, within, and out of the system? What energy transformations occur?

Magnetic Potential Energy

Think about all the different toys or devices that use magnets for entertainment. Many toy building sets use magnets to hold pieces together. Magnets can also be used to make items move or levitate without the cause being known or seen. Magnets are also an important part of many motors, which are used in a variety of devices, such as remote-controlled cars.

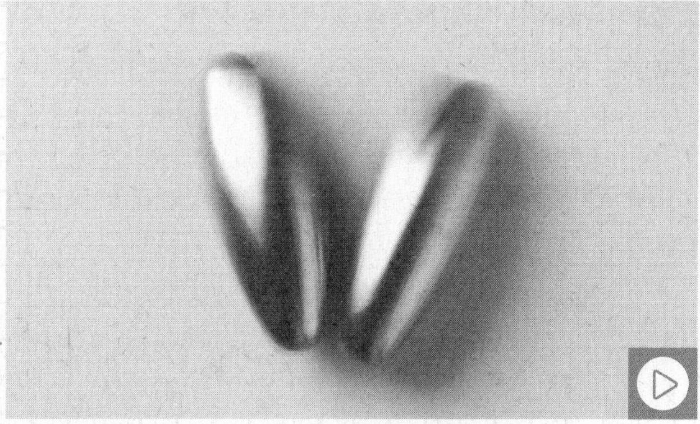

When these magnets move together, they vibrate and even "sing."

8. The photo shows gravitational / magnetic potential energy being transformed into kinetic / potential energy and magnetic / sound energy.

Elastic Potential Energy

Unlike gravitational and magnetic potential energy, elastic potential energy does not depend on a field. Instead, the amount of elastic potential energy an object has depends on the state of the object itself. A catapult, a trampoline, and even an archer's bow all use elastic materials to store elastic potential energy. An elastic material is one that can return to its original state after being stretched or compressed. Springs and rubber bands are common examples of elastic materials. A force can be applied to an elastic material to stretch or compress the material. When the material is allowed to return to its original state, it can then apply a force and transfer energy to another object. This property can be used to do work and make toys and other objects move, bounce, and fly.

9. The toy in the photo can be analyzed as a system. Winding the toy by turning the key tightens a spring. When the key is released, the spring unwinds and the toy moves. How is energy being stored in this system? What causes the potential energy to be transformed into kinetic energy?

Chemical Potential Energy

Many toys are powered by the chemical potential energy in batteries. This energy is transformed into electrical energy that may then be transformed into light or sound. Sometimes, the electrical energy is used to power a motor. Within the motor, the flowing electrical energy interacts with magnets to make parts of the motor turn.

EVIDENCE NOTEBOOK

10. Describe how energy is related to the height a ball reaches when it bounces. Record your evidence.

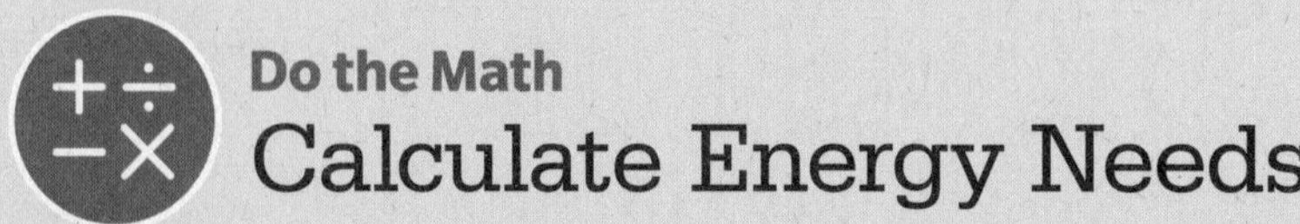

Do the Math

Calculate Energy Needs

The equation to calculate the gravitational potential energy (GPE) of an object is GPE = mgh. In this equation, m is the mass of the object in kilograms, g is the acceleration due to Earth's gravity (9.8 m/s^2), and h is the height of the object above the ground in meters. Energy is expressed in joules (kg · m^2/s^2).

11. Suppose you are designing the launch system for the roller coaster in the diagram. The launch system transfers energy to the cars to begin the ride. If the cars have enough energy to make it over the first hill, the cars can complete the course. The first hill is 61 m higher than the station. The mass of the empty cars is 550.5 kg. The cars can carry up to 12 people, each with a mass of 150 kg. What are the least amounts of energy the launch system must transfer to the cars when they are empty and when they are full to make sure the cars have enough energy to complete the course?

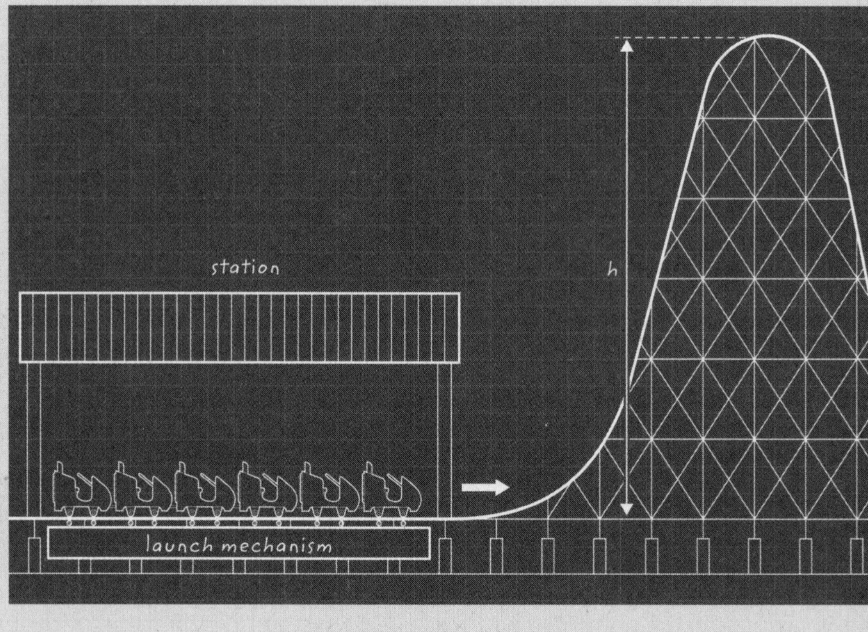

Building a Device to Demonstrate the Transformation of Potential Energy

The Design Process

How do we make roller coasters safer? How do we launch a probe to Saturn? How can we improve medical imaging technology? How do we make computers faster? The engineering design process can be used to solve many problems. It is an iterative process, which means its steps are repeated as needed to find the best possible solution to a problem. The best solution will be the one that best meets the unique criteria for the problem while staying within the constraints, or limitations.

The Engineering Design Process

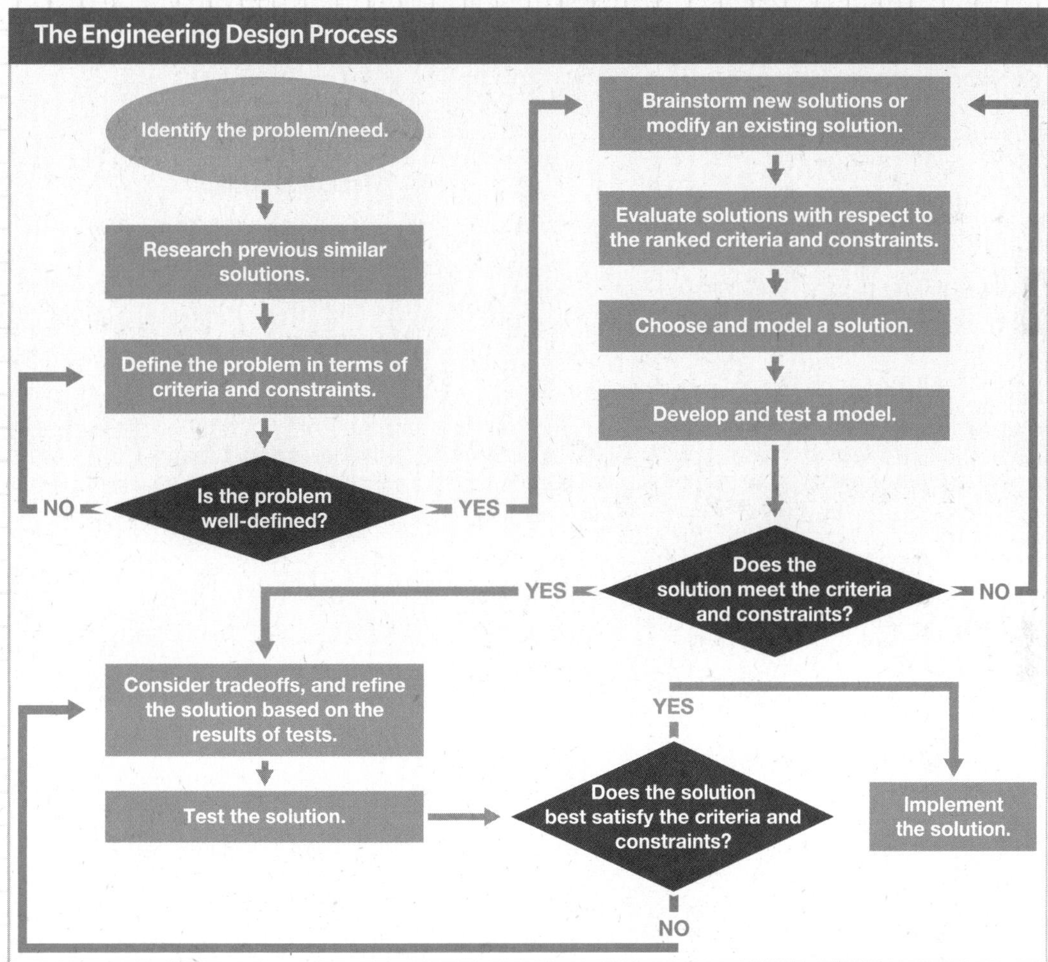

12. The figure shows the engineering design process. What parts of the process give the process flexibility so that it can be used to find solutions to different problems?

Hands-On Lab

Design a Toy to Teach Potential Energy

You will design a toy that will introduce children aged 8–10 years to potential energy. The device should demonstrate different forms and amounts of potential energy.

MATERIALS

- balloons, non-latex
- blocks, wooden
- cardboard tubes
- coins
- craft sticks
- dominoes
- dowels, wooden
- glue, white
- magnets
- marbles
- modeling clay
- rubber bands, non-latex
- skewers, wooden
- straws
- string
- tape
- toy car tracks
- wire, copper, bare

Procedure and Analysis

STEP 1 Complete the list of criteria and constraints to define the design problem. Add one additional criterion and one additional constraint to the table.

Criteria	Constraints
The device • is usable by children aged 8–10 years • is usable by someone who has never used the device before • shows at least one form of potential energy in addition to gravitational potential energy • demonstrates at least two different amounts of the same form of potential energy • transforms potential energy into kinetic energy	The device must • be built during class • be built using the materials provided in class

STEP 2 Research possible solutions for this design problem. Brainstorm additional possible solutions based on your knowledge of potential energy and how it can be transferred and transformed. Record possible solutions on a separate sheet of paper.

STEP 3 Choose the design you believe is the most promising based on the criteria and constraints. Draw a diagram of the design in the space below.

STEP 4 Describe your solution. Explain in detail why you believe the design you chose is the best possible solution. Describe how energy is transferred and transformed in your design.

STEP 5 Build a prototype of your chosen design using the available materials. You will test this prototype in the next part of this lesson.

Choose a Design to Prototype

Before you can do more rigorous testing, you must choose a design to prototype from the designs you brainstormed. Use your knowledge of scientific principles to decide which design you think is most likely to meet your criteria within your given constraints.

13. Which of the following designs is most likely to satisfy the criteria and constraints?

Criteria and Constraints
1. The device helps the user wake up at a specific time.
2. The device does not interfere with the user's sleep.
3. The device is safe for the user.
4. The user can specify the time the device turns on.
5. The device is easily reset.

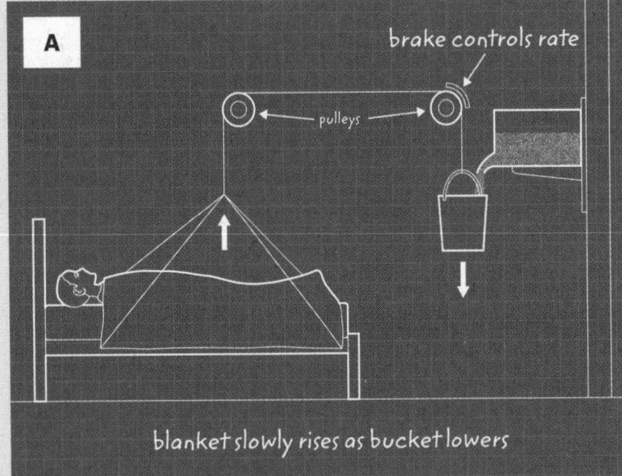

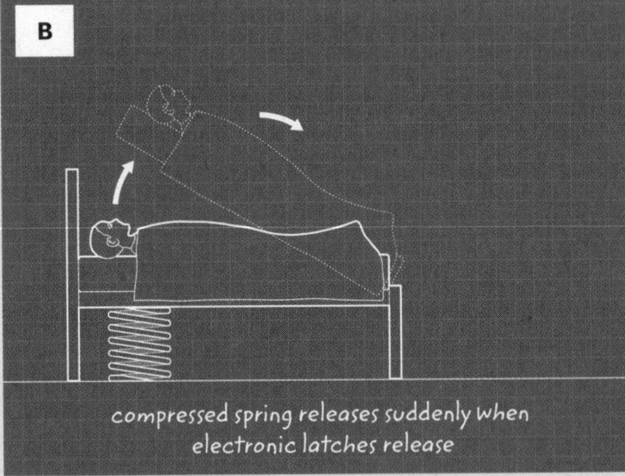

B
compressed spring releases suddenly when electronic latches release

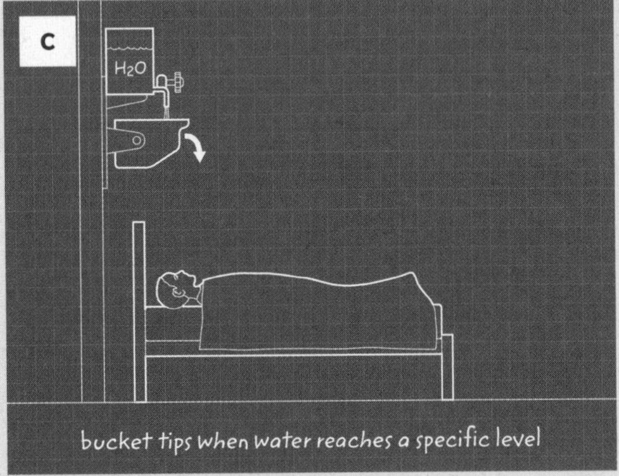

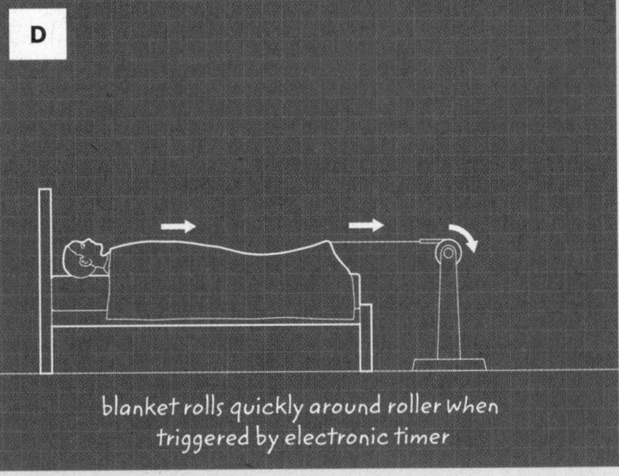

D
blanket rolls quickly around roller when triggered by electronic timer

14. Consider the five criteria and constraints listed in the table. Which one indicates that you should consider the potential energy of the system when selecting the most promising solution? Explain your reasoning.

Testing, Evaluating, and Optimizing a Device

Use Science to Make Design Decisions

As you design a solution to a problem you make many decisions. It is important to use scientific practices to help make these decisions. Basing your decisions on science, rather than on random guessing, will lead to a satisfactory solution more quickly because your decisions will be more likely to have the desired effect.

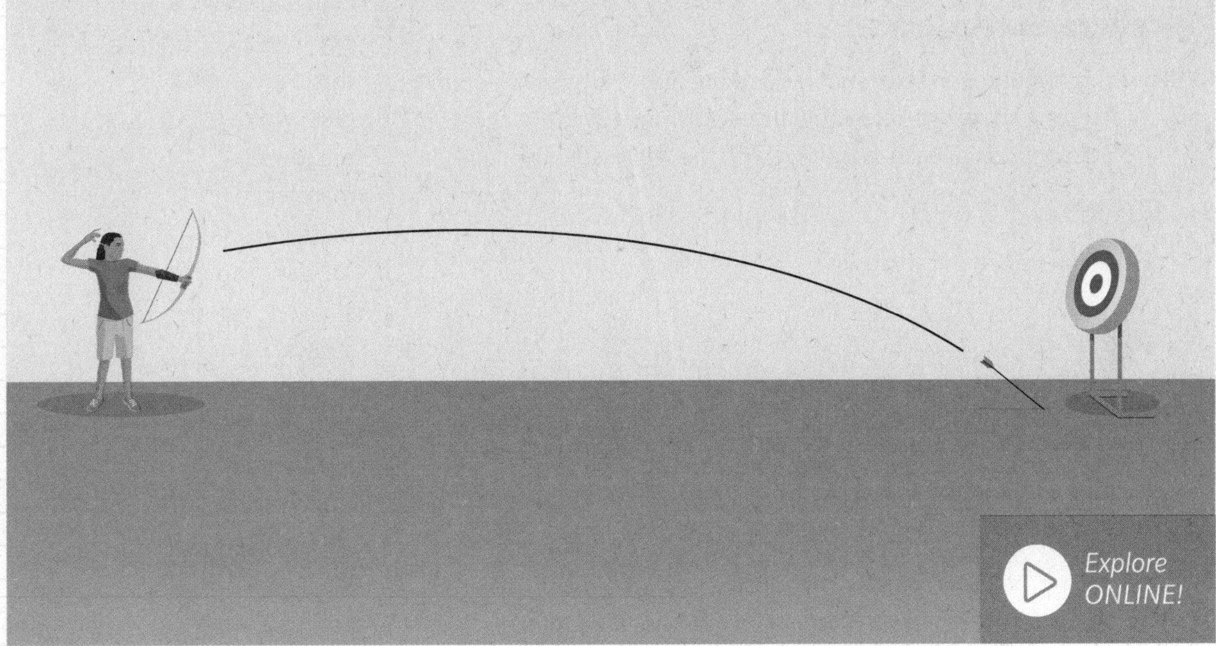

The archer correctly aims the arrow at the target. When she shoots, though, the arrow falls short.

15. The arrow did not reach the target because there was too much / little energy in the system. The archer should pull the string of the bow back more / less to increase / decrease the gravitational / elastic potential energy in the system.

Evaluate and Optimize a Solution

How do you know when a solution is acceptable? You must test the solution and evaluate whether or not it meets your design criteria, given your constraints. Some criteria may be more challenging to measure than others. For example, determining how much fun a design is or assessing usability can be difficult to measure quantitatively. You must develop a method to measure and evaluate your solution's performance for each criterion.

Imagine that you have a solution that satisfies all of your criteria and constraints. Is this the best solution you can develop? Maybe not. In many cases, the design or process may be modified to better meet certain criteria. As with your original design decisions, you should base your modifications on scientific principles. After making a change, the design must be retested to make sure that all of the criteria and constraints are still met. This process may be repeated until the solution has the best performance that is possible for all the criteria. This is the optimized solution.

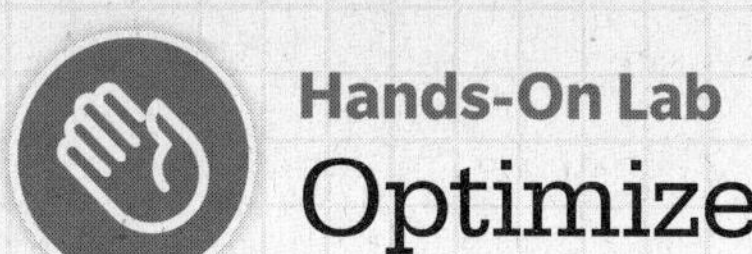

Hands-On Lab

Optimize a Toy to Teach Potential Energy

You will evaluate the prototype you built in the previous part of this lesson. You will determine how well your toy satisfies the criteria within the given constraints. Then you will redesign the toy to improve it. Finally, you must test the redesigned toy to verify that the performance is improved.

MATERIALS

- balloons, non-latex
- blocks, wooden
- cardboard tubes
- coins
- craft sticks
- dominoes
- dowels, wooden
- glue, white
- magnets
- marbles
- modeling clay
- rubber bands, non-latex
- skewers, wooden
- straws
- string
- tape
- toy car tracks
- wire, copper, bare

Procedure and Analysis

STEP 1 Test your toy to see if it works as expected. Perform multiple tests, and record data about its performance. Write a short description of each test along with the test results.

STEP 2 Analyze the test results. How well does your toy meet each criterion? Is the design within the constraints specified?

STEP 3 Describe a change you will make to improve the performance of your toy. Give a short explanation of why the change should improve performance.

STEP 4 Implement the changes described in Step 3, and rerun all of the tests from Step 1 on your redesigned toy. Record data about the performance of the toy.

STEP 5 Analyze the test results of the redesigned toy. Based on these results, does the toy now better satisfy the criteria and constraints?

STEP 6 Is the toy a satisfactory solution to this design problem? Do you think the toy could be further improved? Explain why or why not.

EVIDENCE NOTEBOOK

16. How can a system be adjusted to change the amount of potential energy to bounce a ball higher or lower? Record your evidence.

17. Language SmArts | Create an Advertisement Recall that your toy is meant to introduce children aged 8–10 years to potential energy. Create a magazine advertisement to market the device to these children.

Optimize the Design of a Balloon-Powered Boat

The girl adds potential energy to the balloon-powered boat system by inflating the balloon. When the boat is in the water, the balloon pushes air backwards through the spout, and the air pushes the boat forward. The potential energy in the system transforms into kinetic energy. Once most of the air has been expelled, the boat coasts to a stop. It is desirable that the boat travel as far as possible.

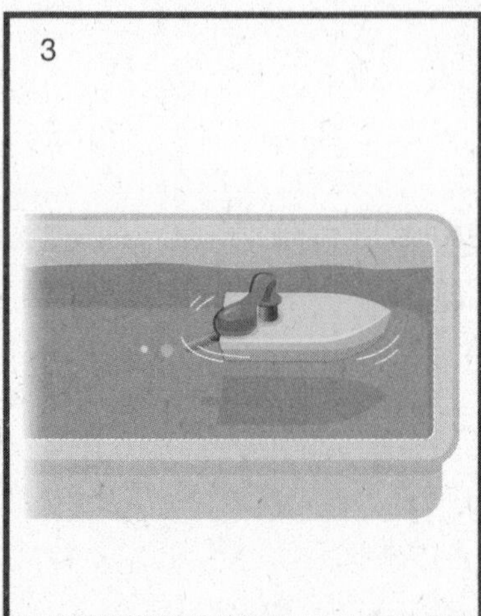

18. How could you modify the boat to improve how far it travels? Explain how this change will help.

Continue Your Exploration

Name: Date:

Check out the path below or go online to choose one of the other paths shown.

People in Engineering

- Hands-On Labs
- Potential Energy in Power and Transportation
- Propose Your Own Path

Go online to choose one of these other paths.

Steve Okamoto, Roller Coaster Designer

Steve Okamoto has been fascinated by roller coasters ever since he first rode on one. So he studied mechanical engineering and studio art and eventually became a product designer. Designing roller coasters is a complex job, so Steve works with a team to design safe and exciting rides.

Roller coasters are large structures that require solid foundations. Civil engineers are experts in designing these foundations. Modern roller coasters often incorporate many electronics to monitor the motion of the cars and to control safety mechanisms. Electrical engineers make sure that the proper electrical components are selected. As a mechanical engineer, Steve may design motors to run the chain lift that raises the cars to the top of the hill. Some roller coasters use magnets or compressed air to transfer energy to the roller coaster cars to begin the ride. These launching mechanisms must also be carefully designed to ensure a safe ride. As an artist, Steve can also make sure the ride is visually appealing so that people want to ride the coaster.

Steve Okamoto and Steel Dragon 2000, a roller coaster that Steve helped design. The cars are just passing the peak of the first hill, the highest point of the roller coaster.

Continue Your Exploration

1. What might be some criteria and constraints for designing a roller coaster?

2. In a traditional gravity coaster, the cars are raised by a chain lift to the top of the first hill. This adds energy to the cars and passengers. The cars are then pulled by gravity to complete the course. How does the amount of energy of the cars and passengers at the top of the first hill relate to the amount of energy during the rest of the ride?

3. What factors might limit the amount of energy that can be added to the cars and passengers of a roller coaster?

4. **Collaborate** With a partner, discuss the skills and knowledge necessary for designing a roller coaster. How might these same skills and knowledge be used to design other devices?

Can You Explain It?

Name: Date:

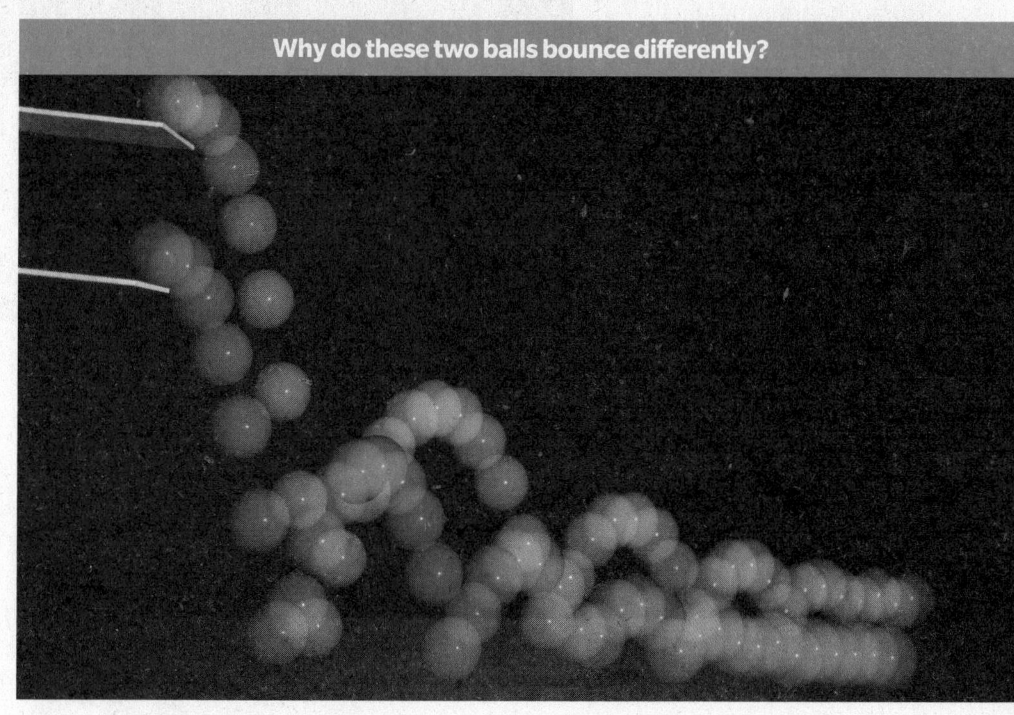
Why do these two balls bounce differently?

Explore ONLINE!

EVIDENCE NOTEBOOK

Refer to the notes in your Evidence Notebook to help you construct an explanation for why the balls bounce differently.

1. State your claim. Make sure your claim fully explains why the balls bounce differently.

2. Summarize the evidence you have gathered to support your claim and explain your reasoning.

Checkpoints

Answer the following questions to check your understanding of the lesson.

Use the diagram to answer Question 3.

3. The satellite in the diagram has gravitational potential energy because of which of the following? Circle all that apply.

A. It has mass.

B. It is moving around Earth.

C. It has height above Earth's surface.

D. It is attracted by gravity toward Earth.

Use the diagram to answer Questions 4–6.

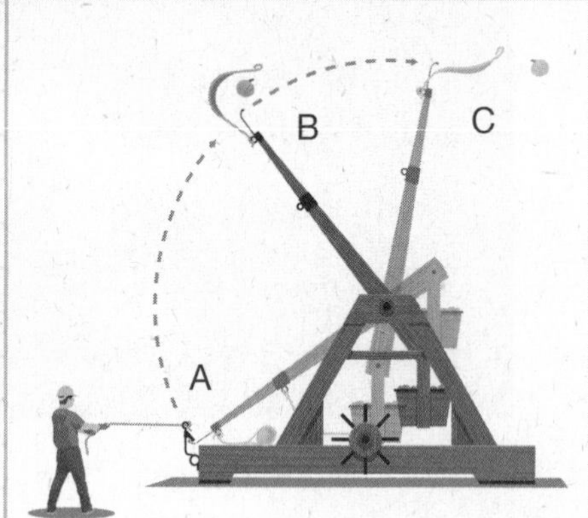

4. When the latch of the trebuchet system is released, gravity pulls the massive counterweight down. As the counterweight moves toward the ground, some of the potential energy of the system is transferred / transformed into kinetic energy. As the throwing arm pulls the sling, the sling applies a force to the payload and transfers / transforms energy to the payload.

5. Which of the following would increase the amount of potential energy stored in the trebuchet system before it is launched? Circle all that apply.

A. Use a counterweight with a greater mass.

B. Use a counterweight of the same mass but different shape.

C. Use a counterweight with less mass.

D. Raise the counterweight higher.

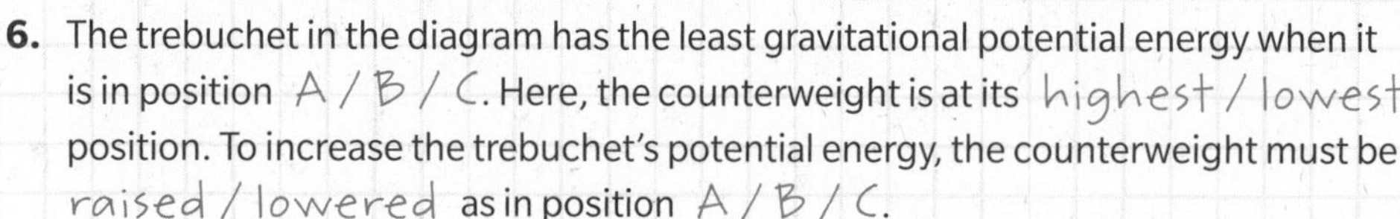

6. The trebuchet in the diagram has the least gravitational potential energy when it is in position A / B / C. Here, the counterweight is at its highest / lowest position. To increase the trebuchet's potential energy, the counterweight must be raised / lowered as in position A / B / C.

---

7. You are testing a water heater design. One criterion is that the water heater heat water to a temperature of 180 °F. During testing, you find that the water in the water heater reaches a temperature of 200 °F. What would you do next?

A. Nothing. It is better for the water to be hotter.

B. Change the criterion to match the test results.

C. Reduce the amount of energy transferred to the water to decrease its temperature and satisfy the criterion.

D. Modify the design to increase the water temperature as much as possible.

Interactive Review

Complete this section to review the main concepts of the lesson.

Potential energy can be transformed into other forms of energy for many tasks. Changing the positions or states of the objects in a system may change the amount of potential energy in a system.

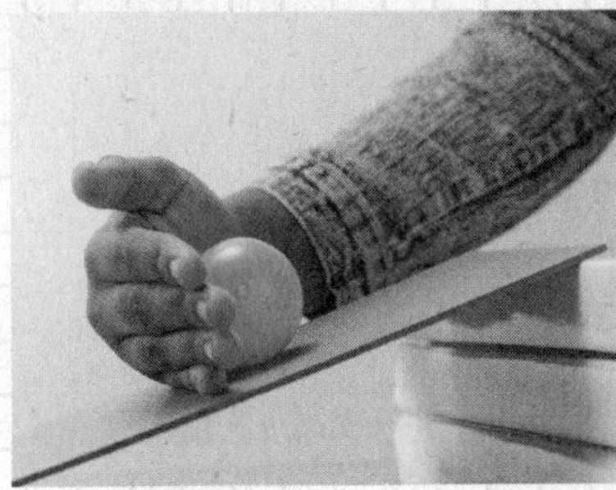

A. What are two ways to increase the potential energy of a system?

The engineering design process is an iterative process that can be used to solve a variety of real-life problems.

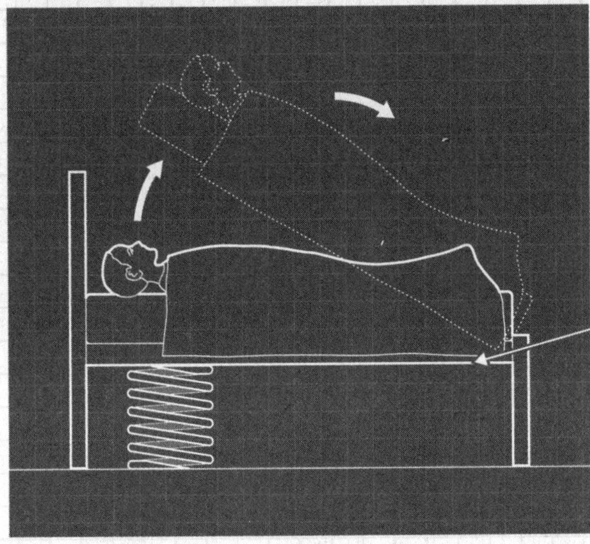

B. Explain how criteria and constraints are used in the engineering design process.

Devices that are built to solve problems may be tested, evaluated, and optimized using the engineering design process and scientific practices.

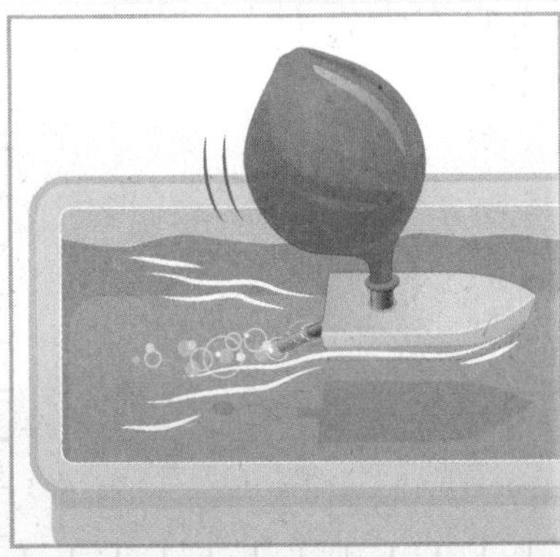

C. Give an example of how the energy of a device might be evaluated and optimized.

Choose one of the activities to explore how this unit connects to other topics.

☐ Engineer It

The Bat's Sweet Spot Baseball and softball players know that when they strike a ball at the "sweet spot" the ball really takes off. What makes a certain part of a bat the sweet spot? What happens if the player doesn't hit the sweet spot? It all relates to energy!

Research where the sweet spot is on a bat and how baseball or softball bats are designed and made. Then, design a better bat. Draw a diagram of your new and improved bat. Consider how different materials could affect its performance. Include a brief written explanation of what happens in terms of energy when a player strikes the ball at the sweet spot or another part of the bat.

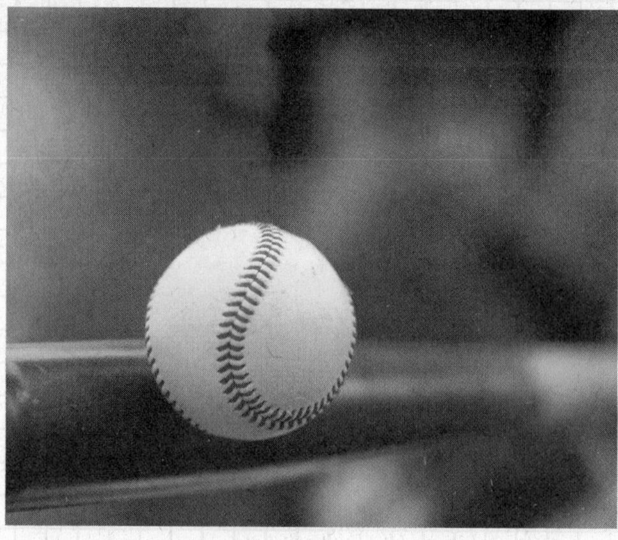

☐ Environmental Science Connection

Green Energy There is a great deal of talk about green energy. But what exactly does it mean? Why is green energy such a hot topic? One example of green energy is wind energy. Large wind turbines are being built to harness energy from wind for use in businesses and homes.

Research sources of green energy and choose one example to explore further. Prepare a diagram of how the energy is generated, describing the transfers and transformations of energy involved.

☐ Social Studies Connection

Harnessing Water Power Waterfalls are amazing and often breath-taking phenomena. They can be relatively small and gentle, causing water to tumble down a stream, or huge and thunderous, dropping hundreds of feet. Humans have long harnessed the hydraulic power in water to turn wheels in mills along rivers. But big changes came when people began to utilize the power of water to generate electrical energy.

The first widely successful hydroelectric power plant was built at Niagara Falls. Research the history of this pioneering engineering feat, and describe how power from the water is transformed into electrical energy for millions of people. Present your findings in a storyboard that you share with your class.

This photo shows a large turbine inside the Niagara Falls power plant when it was first built in 1924.

Name: Date:

Complete this review to check your understanding of the unit.

Use the diagram to answer Questions 1–3.

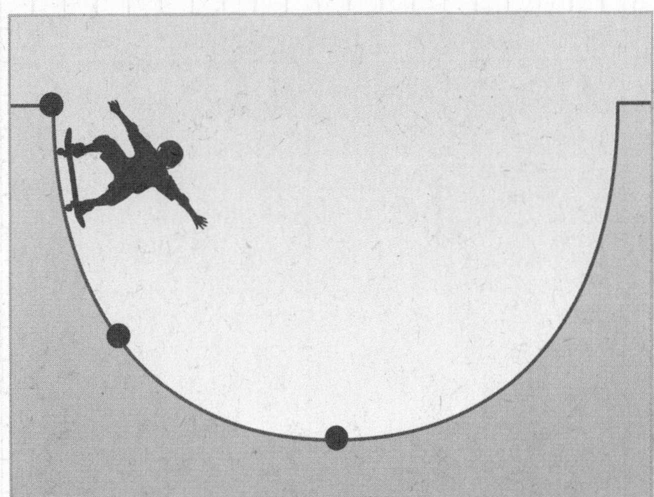

1. At which point on the half-pipe track does the skater have the most potential energy?
   - **A.** Point A
   - **B.** Point B
   - **C.** Point C
   - **D.** The skater's potential energy is the same at all points on the track.

2. Which of the following statements are true? Choose all that apply.
   - **A.** The skater's potential energy decreases as he moves from point A to point C.
   - **B.** The skater's kinetic energy increases as he moves from point A to point C.
   - **C.** The skater's kinetic energy does not change as he moves from point A to point C.
   - **D.** The skater has maximum potential energy at point C.

3. What eventually happens if the skater rides the half-pipe without adding energy to his skateboard by pushing with his feet?
   - **A.** He will continue to move back and forth from one side to the other indefinitely.
   - **B.** He will gradually come to a stop at point C.
   - **C.** He will continue to move back and forth indefinitely but not all the way to the top of each ramp.
   - **D.** He will come to an immediate stop at either point A or point C.

Use the chart to answer Questions 4 and 5.

Record-Setting Sports Speeds

Object	Motion	Speed (m/s)	Mass (g)
Football	Pass	27	425
Tennis ball	Serve	73	59
Baseball	Pitch	47	145

4. The information in the table can be used to calculate which of the following for each object?
   - **A.** kinetic energy
   - **B.** potential energy
   - **C.** neither kinetic or potential energy
   - **D.** both kinetic and potential energy

5. The kinetic energy / gravitational potential energy of an object is directly proportional to its mass and proportional to the square of its velocity. The kinetic energy / gravitational potential energy of an object is directly proportional to its mass and proportional to its height. An object may / may not have both kinetic energy and gravitational potential energy at the same time.

6. Complete the table by providing at least one example of how the following activities relate to each big concept.

System / Activity	Energy Input	Energy Transfer or Transformation	Energy Output
Playing guitar	Plucking a string		
Jumping on a trampoline			
Swinging			
Burning a match			

Name: **Date:**

Use the diagram to answer Questions 7–10.

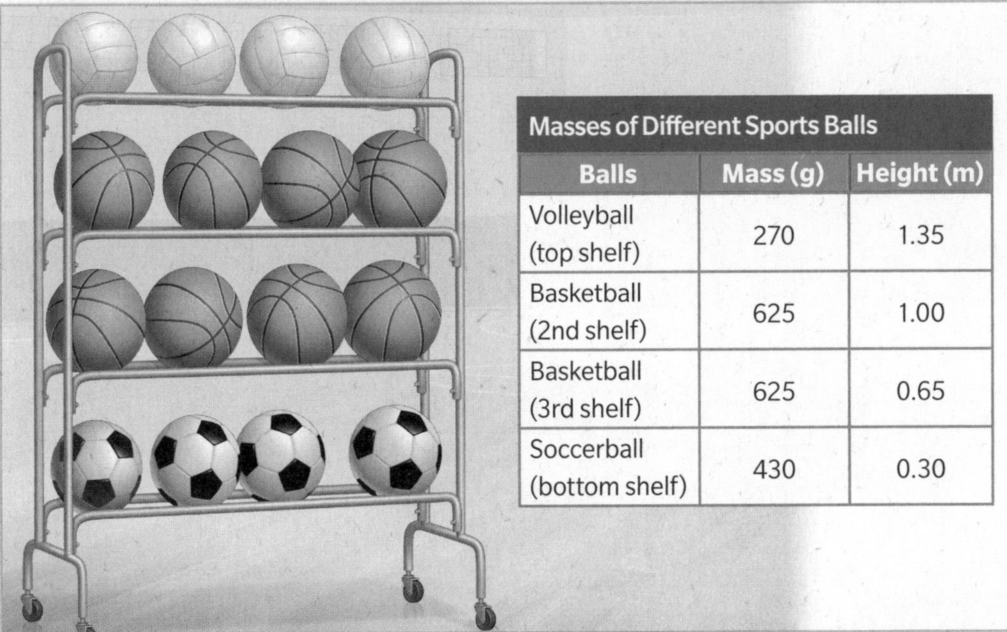

Masses of Different Sports Balls		
Balls	**Mass (g)**	**Height (m)**
Volleyball (top shelf)	270	1.35
Basketball (2nd shelf)	625	1.00
Basketball (3rd shelf)	625	0.65
Soccerball (bottom shelf)	430	0.30

7. What type of energy do the balls have as they rest on the cart? Explain your answer.

8. Which basketballs have the most potential energy, those on the second shelf or those on the third shelf? Explain your reasoning.

9. Do the volleyballs or soccerballs have more potential energy? Explain how you reached your conclusion.

10. A ball that drops from a shelf will bounce several times, with each bounce decreasing in height until the ball comes to rest. Describe the energy transformations that take place. What is happening to the kinetic energy carried by the ball? Where does the kinetic energy go?

Use the images of the hammers to answer Questions 11–14.

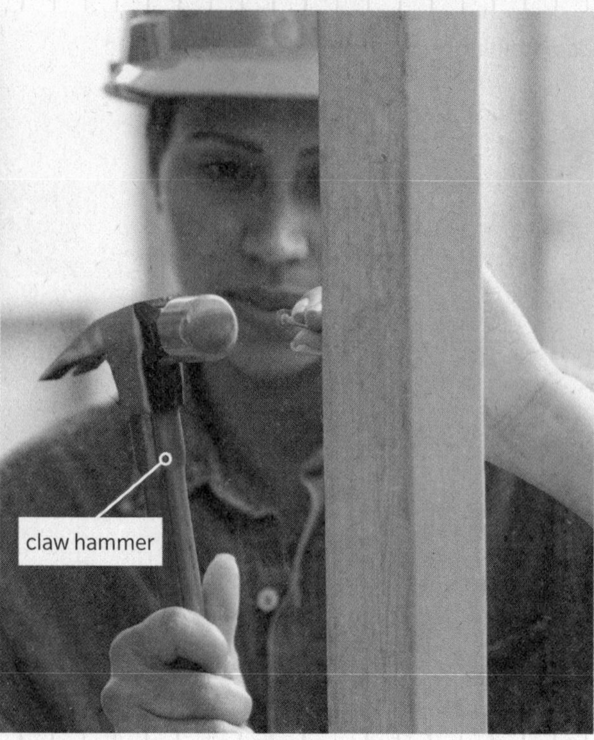

11. Describe the transfer and transformation of energy involved in using a hammer.

12. Which of the hammers shown requires more work to use? Explain your reasoning.

13. Which hammer will be able to do more work? Explain your reasoning.

14. Why are different types of hammers used to accomplish different tasks? Why might a sledgehammer or a claw hammer be inappropriate for certain types of tasks? Explain your reasoning.

Name: Date:

How do energy-storing trains work?

With an ever-growing population and greater energy needs, sometimes power plants simply cannot produce enough electrical energy to meet high energy demands. As a result, the power goes out. Power storage systems using water pumps have been in use for nearly a century, but engineers recently developed a clever new way to store energy involving trains! Potential energy stored in the trains can be used to generate electrical energy when the demand is high.

You are a member of a team of engineers tasked with selling the idea of energy-storing trains to a solar energy company. Prepare a presentation that includes a diagram explaining how energy-storing trains work and why they are ideal solutions for renewable energy systems.

The steps below will help guide you to understand how energy-storing trains work.

Engineer It

1. **Conduct Research** Research energy-storing trains. Briefly explain how these systems work.

Engineer It

2. **Define a Problem** Does the technology exist to create an energy-storing train? What other considerations may affect the ability to create an energy-storing train system?

3. **Develop a Model** Draw a diagram of an energy-storing train system. The model should identify energy inputs, energy outputs, and transformations of energy within the system.

4. **Use the Model** Based on your model, what factors might affect the efficiency of an energy-storing train system?

5. **Communicate your Findings** Prepare a presentation explaining how and why it might be beneficial to combine an energy-storing train system with a solar power system.

Self-Check

	I conducted research on energy-storing trains.
	I identified constraints of the energy-storage problem.
	I developed a model to explain the energy inputs, outputs, and transformations in an energy-storing train system.
	I used the model to identify factors that might affect the efficiency of an energy-storing train system.
	I communicated the benefits of combining an energy-storing train system with a solar power system.

Energy Transfer

An enormous amount of energy is transferred to launch the Orion Multi-Purpose Crew Vehicle into orbit.

Our universe is filled with energy—from the farthest galaxies to our own bodies. Every object has energy, but we tend to only notice it when something is happening—when energy is being transferred from one object to another. What are the different forms of energy? How is energy transferred in systems? In this unit, you will study different forms of energy and learn how energy moves within systems.

Why It Matters

Here are some questions to consider as you work through the unit. Can you answer any of the questions now? Revisit these questions at the end of the unit to apply what you discover.

Questions	Notes
What makes some objects feel colder than others at the same temperature?	
When have you attempted to minimize the change in temperature of an object from hot to cold or cold to hot?	
Why do regions near large bodies of water often have variations in weather from surrounding areas?	
What do we mean when we say a technology is "energy efficient"?	
When have you experienced a change in the form of energy in your everyday life?	

Unit Starter: Investigating Energy Changes in Toast

Study the diagram of the toaster and answer the following questions.

1. When a toaster is in use, electrical energy is transformed into:
   A. light energy only
   B. thermal energy only
   C. thermal and light energy
   D. there are no energy transformations when using a toaster

2. While the toaster is in use, you can feel warmth coming from the outside of the toaster. What would happen if we could keep this thermal energy from transferring out of the toaster? Select all that apply.
   A. The bread would take longer to toast.
   B. There would be more thermal energy available to toast the bread.
   C. There would be less thermal energy available to toast the bread.
   D. The bread would toast faster.

Unit Project

Go online to download the Unit Project Worksheet to help you plan your project.

Cooked to Perfection

Is the sun really hot enough to cook food? Find out when you design and build an oven using only the sun for heat!

LESSON 1

Changes in Energy

China's Three Gorges Dam, the world's largest hydroelectric power station, captures the energy of water and transforms it into electrical energy.

By the end of this lesson . . .

you will be able to demonstrate that a transfer of energy to or from an object results in a change in the total energy of an object.

Go online to view the digital version of the Hands-On Lab for this lesson and to download additional lab resources.

CAN YOU EXPLAIN IT?

How can energy from the motion of the crank on a hand-powered flashlight produce light?

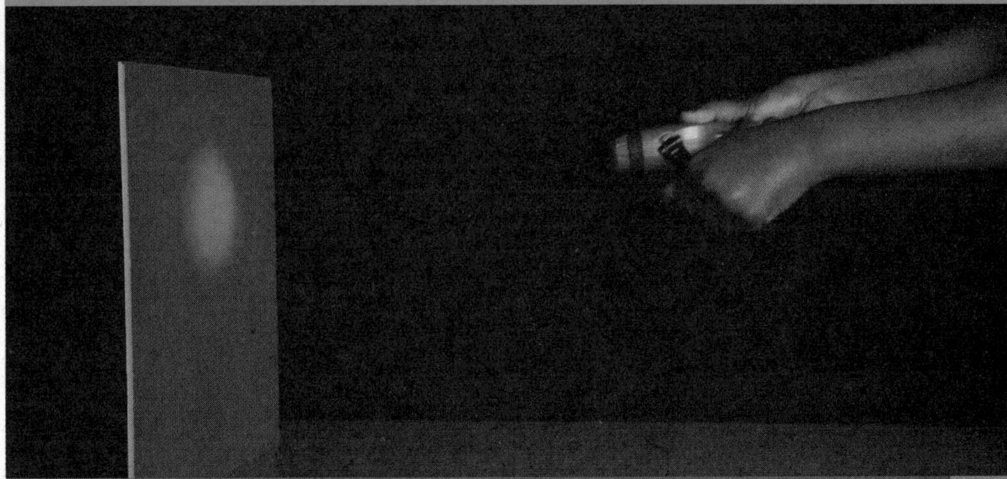

Hand-powered flashlights are useful tools in an emergency. They do not need replaceable batteries or other sources of electric power. Instead, the user turns a crank on the side of the flashlight. This causes the light bulb in the flashlight to light up.

Explore ONLINE!

1. How would you define the flashlight as a system? What are its inputs and outputs? What are the parts of the system?

2. The crank has energy when it is turned. What other types of energy might the flashlight have when the light bulb is on?

EVIDENCE NOTEBOOK As you explore the lesson, gather evidence to help explain how turning the crank of a hand-powered flashlight produces light.

Identifying Different Forms of Energy

Processes and technologies that require energy are all around you. The movement of a clock's hands, the light from light fixtures, and the sounds made by electronic devices are all results of changes in energy. Applying our understanding of energy allows us to do everything from launching rockets to cooking food.

You can observe many types of energy at a carnival.

3. What types of energy can you identify in the photo of the carnival rides?

The Energy of Objects in Motion: Kinetic Energy

A bowling ball rolling down a lane toward the pins has energy. Evidence of this is the force that would be required to stop the rolling ball. A force was also used to send it rolling toward the pins. The energy that an object has due to its motion is called *kinetic energy*. All moving objects have kinetic energy. A bowling ball traveling down a lane, a skateboarder rolling down a ramp, and water rushing down a river all have kinetic energy.

Energy applied by the bowler started this ball moving.

Kinetic Energy and Mass

A bowling ball has a much greater mass than the tiny ball used in a pinball machine. A bowling ball has a mass of 6 kg. A pinball has a mass of 0.08 kg. Think about what would happen if you rolled these balls down the same bowling lane at the same speed. Would both balls have the same amount of energy? Imagine both balls striking the center pin after they roll down the lane. What would happen?

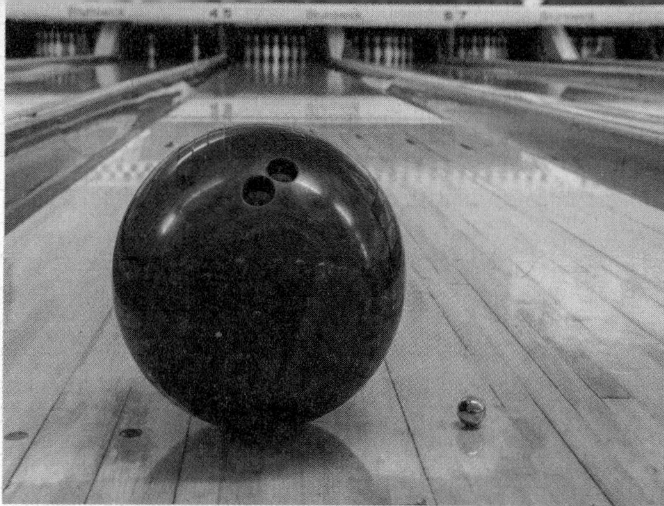

A bowling ball has a much greater mass than a pinball.

4. What evidence could you use to compare the balls' energies? Which ball do you think has more energy?

The kinetic energy of an object depends partly on its mass. In the example above, the bowling ball has more kinetic energy than the pinball. They are traveling at the same speed, but the bowling ball has more mass. You can see that the bowling ball has more kinetic energy because more force is needed to stop the rolling bowling ball.

Kinetic Energy and Speed

Two balls with different masses moving at the same speed have different amounts of kinetic energy. Now think about how different speeds might affect kinetic energy.

5. Two bowlers each roll a 6 kg bowling ball down a lane. One ball rolls very fast. The other rolls slowly. Predict what will happen when each ball reaches the pins. What does your prediction tell you about how much energy each ball has?

Kinetic energy is directly proportional to the mass of an object. It is also proportional to the square of the object's velocity. A ball traveling at a fast speed will require more force to stop its motion than it would if the ball were moving more slowly. Therefore, the ball has more kinetic energy when it is moving faster.

Stored Energy: Potential Energy

A ball at rest at the top of a hill does not have kinetic energy. As it rolls down the hill, it gains kinetic energy. Where does the kinetic energy gained by the ball come from? When the ball is at rest at the top of the hill, its position gives it the potential to begin rolling and gain kinetic energy. The energy stored in an object due to its position or condition is called *potential energy*. For example, increasing the height of this ball's position will increase its potential energy. As the ball rolls down the hill, its potential energy decreases. Its potential energy is as low as possible at the bottom.

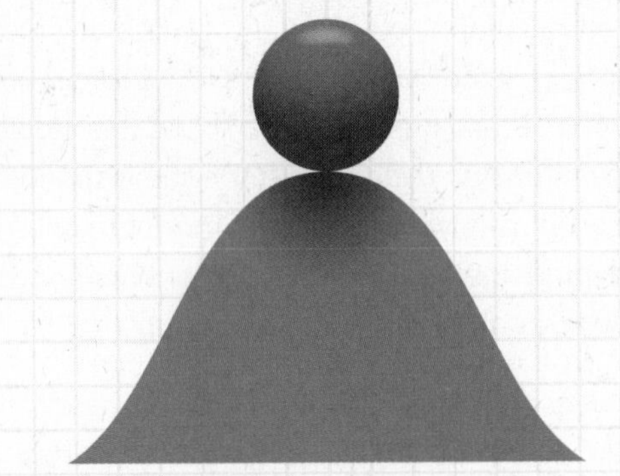

As the ball rolls downhill, its potential energy decreases.

6. In the carnival game in the photo, the player must roll the ball with enough speed to get it over the hill on the track. Think about how the ball's energy changes at different points on the track.

At the top of the hill, the ball's potential energy is at its maximum / minimum.
As the ball rolls downhill, its kinetic energy increases / decreases and its potential energy increases / decreases. At the bottom of the hill, the ball's potential energy is at its maximum / minimum and its kinetic energy is at its maximum / minimum.

The bowling balls in this carnival game have both potential and kinetic energy.

The ball slows down as it rolls uphill. It speeds up as it rolls downhill. As the ball loses potential energy, it gains kinetic energy. When the ball gains potential energy, it loses kinetic energy. The total energy that the ball has does not change. Like matter, energy cannot be created or destroyed. That means that the total amount of energy in a system does not change unless energy is added to it or removed from it. This is known as the *law of conservation of energy*.

Changes in Potential Energy

Just as a ball on a hill will naturally roll downward, the water at the top of a waterfall will flow downward. A pendulum released from the top of its arc will swing downward. Before they move downward, the ball, the water, and the pendulum have potential energy because of their positions.

The potential energy of an object due to its height, or its position relative to Earth's surface, is called *gravitational potential energy*. The higher an object is, the greater its gravitational potential energy. For example, water at the top of a waterfall will have its greatest gravitational potential energy because its height above Earth's surface is greater than it is at the bottom of the waterfall.

Think about water flowing down a waterfall. Its energy changes as it moves from the top to the bottom of the falls. How can you describe the general behavior of objects undergoing changes in potential energy?

7. Objects tend to move from places where they have more / less potential energy to places where they have more / less potential energy. In other words, changes in energy tend to result in a(n) increase / decrease in potential energy.

Imagine holding a ball in the air. If you drop it, the ball will fall to the ground. It falls due to the pull of Earth's gravity. All objects tend to move from places where they have higher gravitational potential energy to places where they have lower gravitational potential energy. This means that balls do not roll uphill on their own. Pendulums do not spontaneously swing upward. Water does not flow up a waterfall on its own. However, you can make objects move upward by adding energy to them.

As water at the top of the waterfall flows downward, its potential energy decreases.

Forms of Energy

All energy is either potential energy or kinetic energy. Potential energy is due to an object's position or condition. Kinetic energy results from an object's motion. Each type of energy comes in different forms. Thermal energy, sound energy, electromagnetic energy, and electrical energy are forms of kinetic energy. Chemical energy, nuclear energy, gravitational potential energy, and elastic potential energy are forms of potential energy. All forms of energy are expressed in units of joules (J).

Mechanical Energy

Mechanical energy describes an object's ability to move—or do work on—other objects. It is the sum of the potential energy and kinetic energy of an object or a system. For example, a person swinging a hammer is providing kinetic energy to the hammer. The hammer does work on a nail. An object's mechanical energy can be all potential energy. It can be all kinetic energy. It can also be a combination of the two.

A hammer provides mechanical energy to do work on a nail.

Other Forms of Energy

You use many forms of energy every day. In fact, you are using several forms of energy as you explore this lesson! Electrical energy is a flow of negatively charged particles that creates the electric current used to power computers, lamps, toasters, and other technologies. Chemical energy is the form of energy involved in chemical reactions. The battery on your cell phone uses chemical energy. Nuclear energy powers the sun. The sun gives off light energy that reaches Earth.

More than one form of energy can exist in a system at the same time. For example, fireworks explode because a huge amount of chemical potential energy is released. This energy becomes sound, light, and thermal energy.

Electromagnetic energy is a form of energy that can travel though space in the form of waves. Electromagnetic waves include visible light, x-rays, microwaves, and radio waves.

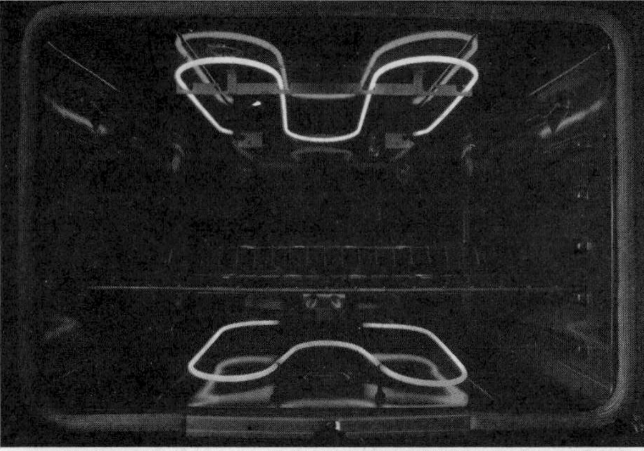

Thermal energy is the kinetic energy of the particles that make up matter. The faster the molecules in an object move, the more thermal energy the object has. As its thermal energy increases, an object will feel warmer.

Sound energy is kinetic energy caused by the vibrations of the particles that make up the matter in a solid, liquid, or gas. As the particles vibrate, they transfer the sound energy to other particles. Your ears pick up the vibrations of particles in the air, which you hear as sound.

EVIDENCE NOTEBOOK

8. Think about the hand-cranked flashlight. What kinds of energy are involved in the operation of the flashlight? Record your evidence.

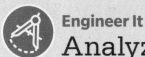

Engineer It

Analyze Applications of Mechanical Energy

Throughout history, people have designed machines that made the seemingly impossible possible. Many of these tools do work to increase the potential energy of an object or system. A simple lever can be used to lift a heavy boulder. Lifting it increases its potential energy. The lever can move the huge rock because the person using the lever adds kinetic energy by pushing the lever.

A towering 25-meter stone pillar called an obelisk stands in the center of St. Peter's Square in Rome. The 320,000-kilogram obelisk was put in place in 1586. The diagram shows how winches, shown as circles, were used. Some 900 workers and 140 horses pushed on levers to turn the winches, winding rope around their barrels. The ropes pulled on the obelisk to lift it into the place where it stands today.

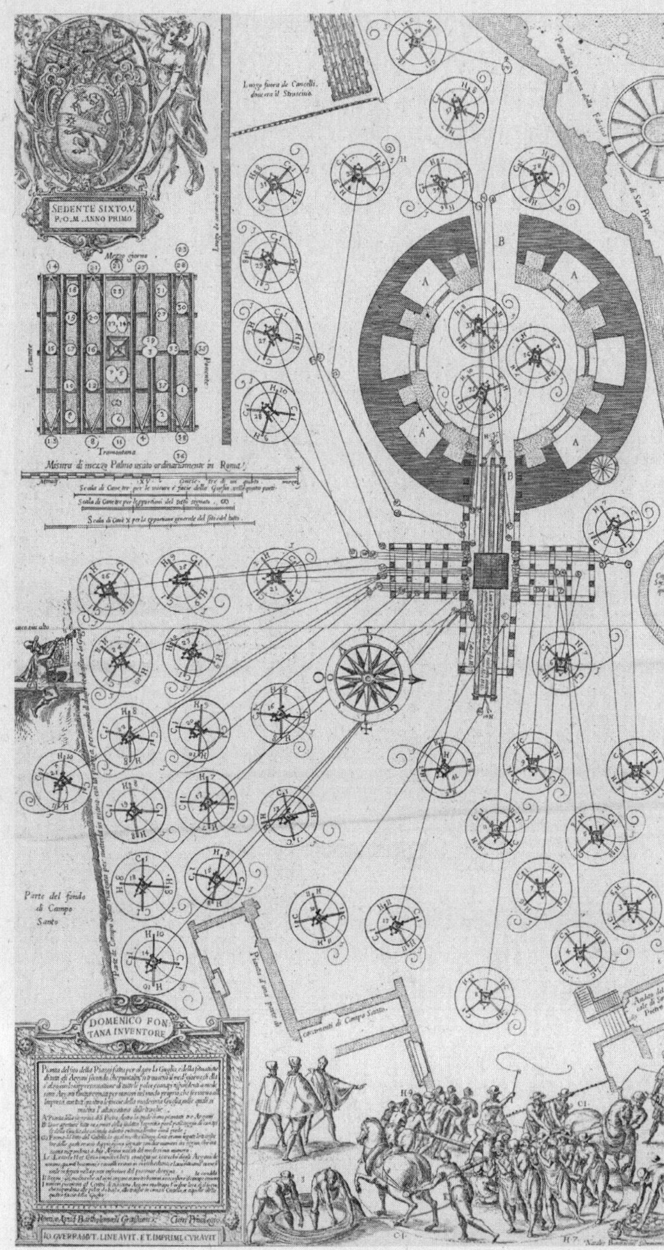

The Vatican Obelisk was first built by the Egyptians 3,200 years ago. This illustration shows how the obelisk was later installed in its current location in St. Peter's Square in Rome.

9. Objects tend to come to rest at a position of lowest potential energy. Think of a machine or system that works against this tendency. Describe how kinetic energy is needed to increase the system's potential energy.

10. How might your machine or system be improved? What constraints might be involved in its design?

Observing Energy Transfer

Recall that all forms of energy fall into two main categories—potential energy and kinetic energy. The position or condition of an object determines its potential energy. The speed and mass of an object determines its kinetic energy. A heavier object has greater kinetic energy than a lighter object moving at the same speed. Likewise, an object moving more quickly has more kinetic energy than a slower object with the same mass.

Think back to a bowling ball rolling down a lane. You know it has kinetic energy because it is moving. As the ball hits the pins, it slows. What happens to the kinetic energy of the bowling ball when it reaches the pins?

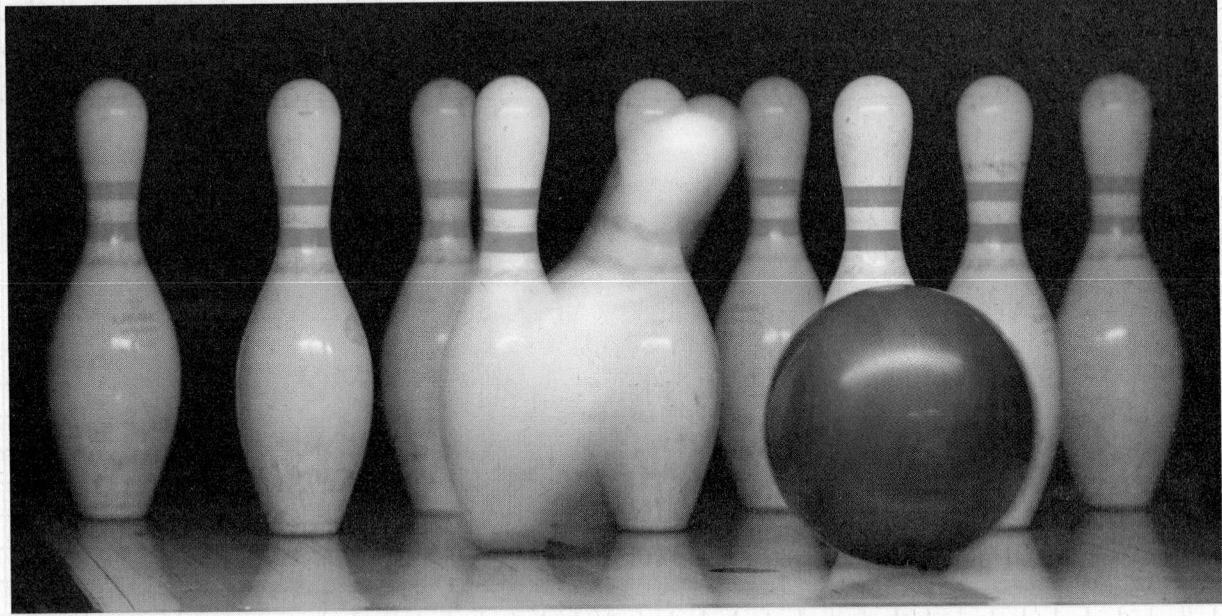

The bowling ball has kinetic energy as it moves toward the pins. The pins scatter in different directions when the ball hits them.

11. Predict what will happen if the ball rolls straight into an object with a greater mass than a bowling pin.

Hands-On Lab

Investigate the Transfer of Energy

You will roll balls with different masses down a ramp at different heights. You will record how these factors affect the distance a cup moves when the balls hit it.

MATERIALS

- balance
- balls, of different masses
- books
- cardboard panel or plastic racecar track
- cup, plastic, with a section of the side cut out
- masking tape
- meterstick

Procedure and Analysis

STEP 1 Stack the books until they are about 20 cm high. Place one end of the cardboard panel or plastic racecar track on the books to make a ramp. Use masking tape to mark a starting point at the top of the ramp. Use a second piece of masking tape to mark a position near the bottom of the ramp where the target cup will be placed.

STEP 2 Use the balance to find the mass of Ball 1. Record the mass in the table below.

Ball	Mass	Distance moved: low ramp	Distance moved: high ramp
1			
2			
3			

STEP 3 Place the target cup with its cut side down on the masking tape. The open top of the cup should face the ramp so it can catch the ball. Release Ball 1 from the starting point at the top of the ramp. Measure the distance the cup moves after it catches the ball. Record your data in the table.

STEP 4 Repeat Steps 2 and 3 with other balls that have different masses.

STEP 5 Add books to the stack to change the slope of the ramp. Repeat Steps 3 and 4.

STEP 6 How did the distance the cup moved change as the mass of the ball changed? How did the distance change as the height of the ramp changed?

STEP 7 **Language SmArts** On a separate sheet of paper, use the results of the activity to construct a statement about how mass and speed affect the transfer of kinetic energy. How can this investigation serve as a model for collisions in the real world?

Energy Transfer in Collisions

Objects that are not moving need energy to set them in motion. They carry that energy with them as they move. They can pass this kinetic energy to other objects when they collide. The passing of energy from one object to another is known as **energy transfer.** Because energy cannot be created or destroyed, you can model energy flowing through a system as inputs and outputs. Think about the bowling ball. It needed an input of energy from the bowler. The ball carried that energy as it rolled down the lane. When the ball collided with a pin, it transferred energy to the pin. Energy is transferred from the object with more kinetic energy to the one with less kinetic energy. The pin moves because energy was transferred to it.

Energy transfers in other types of collisions can also be modeled. For example, energy is transferred within the system when a swinging pendulum hits a pendulum that is not moving. Transferring kinetic energy to an object can move it to a position with higher potential energy.

Energy is transferred from the bowler's hand to the bowling ball. Then it is transferred from the bowling ball to the pin.

Energy Transfer between Objects of the Same Size and Mass

12. Two identical pendulums are set to collide. Identify where the potential energy and kinetic energy of the swinging pendulum are greatest. Then, draw an arrow representing the transfer of energy between the pendulums in the second photo.

• greatest potential energy	• greatest kinetic energy

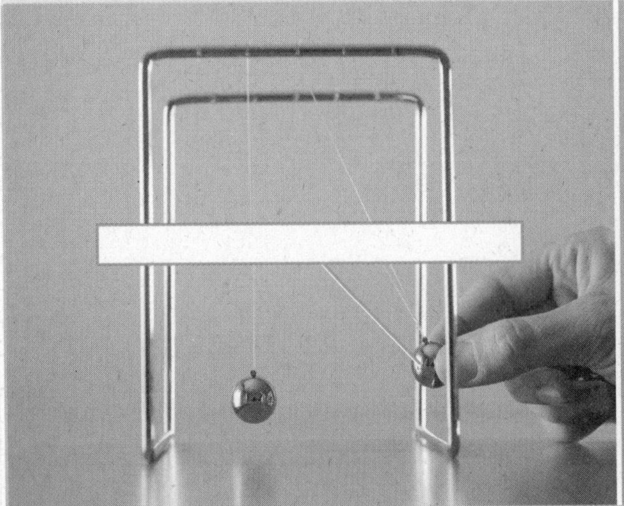

Energy Transfer in Larger Systems

In the pendulum collision, the kinetic energy from the moving pendulum is transferred to the motionless one. The transfer of kinetic energy causes the stationary pendulum to move to a position of greater potential energy than it had at its starting point. That system only had two pendulums. What happens when multiple objects are involved in a transfer of energy within a system? Consider a Newton's cradle, a series of identical pendulums hanging side by side.

Energy Transfer in a Newton's Cradle

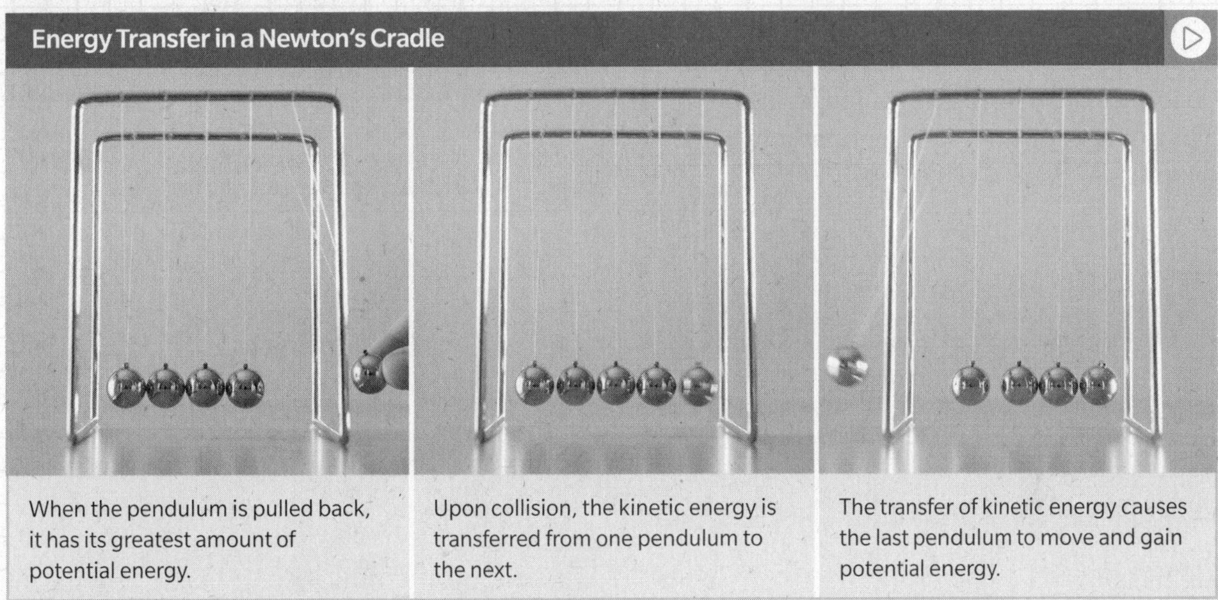

When the pendulum is pulled back, it has its greatest amount of potential energy.	Upon collision, the kinetic energy is transferred from one pendulum to the next.	The transfer of kinetic energy causes the last pendulum to move and gain potential energy.

13. Draw Create a diagram showing the transfer of energy between multiple pendulums within the system of a Newton's cradle.

Water Power

The downward flow of water in a river is the result of the pull of gravity. As water moves downhill, its potential energy transforms into kinetic energy. This energy can be transferred to other objects as well, such as a raft floating down the river. The energy can also be used to do other work, as in a water wheel. A water wheel can be used to turn a gristmill, which uses the energy to grind grains for flour. A water wheel can also be used to power cranes. Cranes use energy from the water to lift and lower objects.

Energy from flowing water is transferred to the water wheel, causing it to turn.

Energy in Machines

Transfers of kinetic energy are used in devices and processes that reduce human effort. They may also improve efficiency. Energy transfer can also be used to do things that the human body alone would not be able to do.

The raising of the obelisk in St. Peter's Square was made possible by the transfer of kinetic energy from many people and animals. Ancient Roman and medieval builders also used human-powered treadwheels to transfer energy. They could power cranes that were used to lift large stones to build temples, castles, and cathedrals.

This 1860 painting by Michele Renault shows workers loading a cargo ship with marble blocks using a treadwheel crane. The hoist was powered by turning the large wheel.

EVIDENCE NOTEBOOK

14. Describe the transfer of kinetic energy that occurs between a person and the crank of a hand-cranked flashlight. Record your evidence.

Analyze Meteoroid Deflection

Stony or metallic space objects known as *meteoroids* often enter Earth's atmosphere. Most are small. They burn up before they reach Earth's surface. Rarely, larger chunks traveling at extremely high speeds hit Earth's surface. Because of their high speeds, the objects have a large amount of kinetic energy. Such an impact can have disastrous results.

In 1908, a 91-million-kilogram space rock entered Earth's atmosphere above Tunguska, Siberia. The rock exploded in the sky, producing a huge fireball that destroyed 2,000 square kilometers of forest. A similar blast happened over another site in Russia in 2013, injuring 1,500 people and damaging thousands of buildings.

This photo shows a portion of the forest destroyed in the aftermath of the Tunguska event.

15. Write One idea for avoiding a catastrophic collision of space debris with Earth is the use of missile-like projectiles to knock the object off course. How can scientists be sure to create an impact with enough kinetic energy to change a meteoroid's course? What factors should they consider?

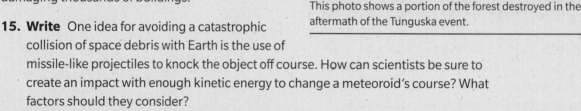

Modeling Energy Transformations

As you observed with the Newton's cradle, kinetic energy is transferred between objects when one object collides with another. However, if you continued to watch the pendulums, you would observe that they gradually swing lower and lower until they eventually come to a stop.

16. Why does the Newton's cradle stop swinging? What does this imply about the energy in the system of pendulums?

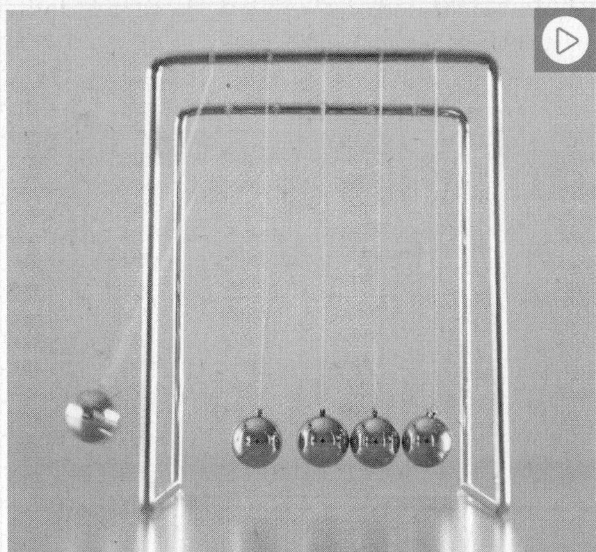

As the action of the Newton's cradle progresses over time, the pendulums gradually slow to a stop.

Transformations: Changes in the Form of Energy

You can see the transfer of mechanical kinetic energy when one pendulum hits another. Energy also seems to be lost gradually from the system as the pendulums lose speed and height with each swing. The final state of the pendulums has less gravitational potential energy than the initial state, because the pendulums come to rest at the lowest point in each of their paths. The law of conservation of energy says that energy cannot be created or destroyed, so the "lost" energy must transfer somewhere else or be changed in some way.

17. Think about collisions and what you know about different forms of energy. What other forms of energy might result from collisions in a Newton's cradle?

When the pendulums collided, they made a sound. This sound is evidence that some of the energy transferred during the collision changed forms. It became sound energy. The collisions also increased the kinetic energy of the particles that make up the pendulums. This increases the thermal energy of the system. The process of one form of energy changing to another form is known as **energy transformation.** It differs from simple energy transfer in which energy moves from one object to another or from one place to another while staying in the same form.

Everyday Uses of Energy Transformations

The process of energy transformation happens all the time and everywhere. In fact, all of the electronic technologies you use every day need energy transformations to work. Refrigerators, microwave ovens, lights, batteries, and cars all rely on energy transformations. They make use of the fact that any form of energy can transform into any other form of energy. For example, a personal music player transforms electrical energy to sound energy and thermal energy.

The chemical energy stored in fireworks is transformed into electromagnetic, sound, and thermal energy.

Electrical energy is transformed into electromagnetic energy and sound energy in a television or computer monitor.

Batteries power electronic devices by transforming chemical energy into electrical energy.

People can also generate electrical energy. Wind-up radios work by converting kinetic mechanical energy from a person to electrical energy.

Alternative Energy and Energy Transformations

Today, many people are looking for energy sources other than fossil fuels. Many alternative energy sources transform kinetic mechanical energy into electrical energy. In hydroelectric dams, the kinetic energy of flowing water is transferred to a turbine that transforms that energy into electricity. Windmills work similarly, using the kinetic energy of wind to generate electricity. Tidal energy provides power by converting the kinetic energy of ocean waves into electrical energy. Solar panels do not use kinetic energy. Instead, they transform light energy from the sun directly into electrical energy.

EVIDENCE NOTEBOOK

18. What types of energy transformation occur during the transfer of energy in the hand-cranked flashlight? Record your evidence.

Energy Loss

Think about a Newton's cradle again. During the collisions, some energy is transferred between the pendulums as mechanical energy. Some energy is also transformed into sound and thermal energy. What happens to the energy that is converted into sound and thermal energy?

19. Draw Reconsider the diagram of energy transfer within the Newton's cradle system you created earlier in this lesson. How would you revise your model to account for the transformations of energy that also occur during the collisions between the pendulums? Where are the additional forms of energy transferred?

The energy from the pendulum collisions that is transformed into sound energy is carried through vibrations of the molecules in the air around the pendulums. The energy that is transformed into thermal energy is also transferred to the surrounding air. With each collision, this energy is transferred away from the Newton's cradle.

Because energy cannot be created or destroyed, transfers of energy away from a system to its surroundings result in an overall loss of energy from the system. The loss of energy from a system may seem minor, but over time it adds up. The motion of the pendulums in a Newton's cradle decreases as the system loses energy. Eventually, the cradle comes to a complete stop. An input of kinetic energy is needed to start the cradle swinging again.

Do the Math | Energy Efficiency The ratio of useful energy to the overall input energy in a system is known as *efficiency*. Incandescent light bulbs are not efficient. They transform a large portion of electrical energy into thermal energy instead of light. To save energy, these bulbs have been replaced with compact fluorescent lamps (CFLs) and light-emitting diodes (LEDs). CFLs and LEDs use less electrical energy to produce the same amount of light.

The flow of energy through a system can be expressed in watts (W). One watt is equal to the flow of one joule of energy for one second. This table shows the wattage of each type of bulb with equivalent brightness. Electrical energy is often measured in kilowatt-hours (kW•h), or the amount of energy used in one hour at the rate of 1,000 W.

Energy Used by Light Bulbs

Bulb type	Watts (J/s)	Energy used over 2,000 hours (kW•h)
Incandescent	60	120
CFL	14	28
LED	10	20

20. Suppose the price of electricity is 12.75 cents per kW•h. What is the difference in cost in dollars between the use of an incandescent bulb for 2,000 hours and an LED bulb for the same amount of time?

21. How much more energy (in J) does an incandescent bulb use than a CFL in one minute?

Describe Efficient Energy Use

Laptops and other electronic devices become warm when they are in use. Some of the chemical energy from the battery is transformed into thermal energy instead of electrical energy. Much of the electrical energy produced by the battery becomes thermal energy as it flows through the computer parts. The electrical energy is useful, but the thermal energy is not. The battery loses chemical energy in both useful and non-useful transformations as it is used.

A laptop battery produces thermal energy.

22. Discuss Hand-cranked flashlights transform mechanical energy into other forms of energy. Which energy transformations are useful, and which are not? Explain why most hand-cranked flashlights are made with LEDs.

Continue Your Exploration

Name: Date:

Check out the path below or go online to choose one of the other paths shown.

Moving Water Uphill

- **Hands-On Labs**
- **Hydroelectric Power**
- **Propose Your Own Path**

Go online to choose one of these other paths.

A water wheel uses kinetic energy from flowing water to power machinery. In this use, mechanical energy supplied by moving water is used to power another process. Another type of water wheel, called a *noria*, is not used to supply mechanical energy for other processes. A noria's only purpose is to raise water to a higher location.

A noria is similar to other water wheels, except that it has open containers along the outer rim of its wheel. The containers fill with water when they are lowered into a body of flowing water, such as a river, as the wheel turns. As the wheel continues to turn, the containers of water are lifted. During this upward movement, the containers overturn and empty the water into a higher trough or aqueduct. The water can then be transported to another location for irrigation or use in towns and villages.

1. Kinetic energy from water flowing in the river is transferred to the noria, which lifts water from the river to the aqueduct. How does the gravitational potential energy of the water change as it approaches the top of the wheel?
   - **A.** Its gravitational potential energy does not change.
   - **B.** Its gravitational potential energy increases.
   - **C.** Its gravitational potential energy decreases.

The norias of Hama, Syria, are the largest in the world. They were used for centuries to lift water from the Orontes River. Today, they are mostly unused.

Continue Your Exploration

As water reaches the top of the wheel, it pours into a collecting trough.

2. The norias of Hama are known for creaking loudly as they turn. Which statements about a noria are correct? Choose all that apply.
   A. Some kinetic energy of the noria is transformed into sound energy.
   B. Some energy of the noria is lost from the system due to friction.
   C. The kinetic energy of the noria does not change.
   D. The noria does not have any input or output of energy.

3. Paddle boats are boats that are propelled by a paddle wheel similar to a water wheel. The paddle can be operated using human power, a steam engine, or solar power. Describe the energy transfer and transformations that take place within the paddle wheel system.

4. **Collaborate** Water wheels can be good sources of renewable energy. Norias help people use water resources. Because these devices rely on running water to function, they are not always reliable. Discuss how the availability of flowing water affects the usefulness of a water wheel. Discuss how you might plan ahead to deal with changes in conditions, such as a drought.

Can You Explain It?

Name: Date:

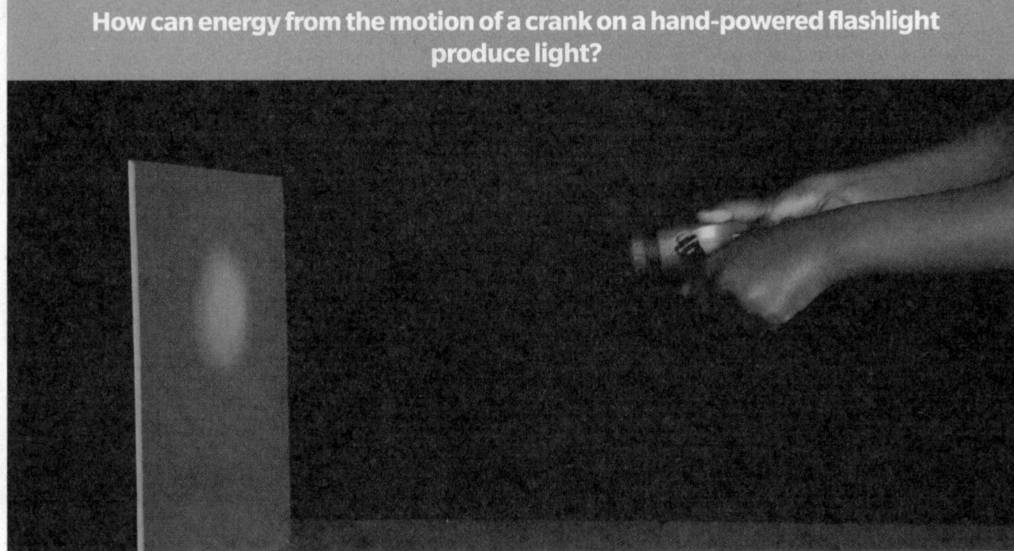
How can energy from the motion of a crank on a hand-powered flashlight produce light?

Explore ONLINE!

EVIDENCE NOTEBOOK

Refer to the notes in your Evidence Notebook to help you construct an explanation for how the input of mechanical energy with the crank is able to produce an output of light.

1. State your claim. Make sure your claim fully explains the transfer and transformation of kinetic energy within the system.

2. Summarize the evidence you have gathered to support your claim and explain your reasoning.

Checkpoints

Answer the following questions to check your understanding of the lesson.

Use the photo of the roller coaster to answer Questions 3 and 4.

3. As the cars move downward on the loop, their kinetic energy decreases / increases. The cars have the greatest amount of potential energy when they are at the bottom / top of the loop.

4. The roller coaster requires an input of energy from a motor to reach the top of the first hill. Which statement describes the transformation of energy involved in this process?

A. Mechanical energy is transformed into electrical energy.

B. Electrical energy is transformed into chemical energy.

C. Electrical energy is transformed into mechanical energy.

D. No energy transformation occurs.

Use the table to answer Question 5.

5. Each of the balls in the table collided with a stationary object of the same mass. Which statements about the transfer of kinetic energy are correct? Choose all that apply.

A. Ball A and Ball B transfer the same amount of energy.

B. Ball B transfers more energy than Ball A.

C. Ball B and Ball C transfer the same amount of energy.

D. Ball C transfers more energy than Ball B.

Ball	Mass (g)	Velocity (m/s)
Ball A	45	30
Ball B	45	40
Ball C	60	40

---

6. When a television is turned on, electrical energy is transformed into which of these forms of energy? Choose all that apply.

A. sound energy

B. thermal energy

C. chemical energy

D. electromagnetic energy

Interactive Review

Complete this interactive study guide to review the lesson.

Kinetic energy is the energy of an object due to its speed and mass. Potential energy is the energy of an object due to its position or condition.

A. Describe how the speed and mass of an object affect the amount of kinetic energy an object possesses.

Changes in kinetic energy involve a transfer of energy to or from an object.

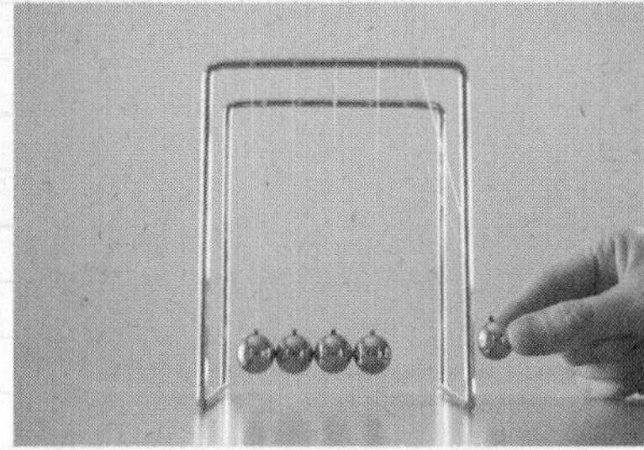

B. Describe the transfer of energy between the pendulums in a Newton's cradle.

A change in energy from one form to another is known as an energy transformation. Any form of energy can transform into any other form of energy.

C. Explain how evidence of energy transformation in fireworks supports the law of conservation of energy.

LESSON 2

Temperature and Heat

Even when the temperature is very cold outside, an insulated coat can keep you warm.

By the end of this lesson . . .

you will be able to explain the relationships between temperature, thermal energy, and heat.

Go online to view the digital version of the Hands-On Lab for this lesson and to download additional lab resources.

CAN YOU EXPLAIN IT?

What allows us to visualize temperature differences?

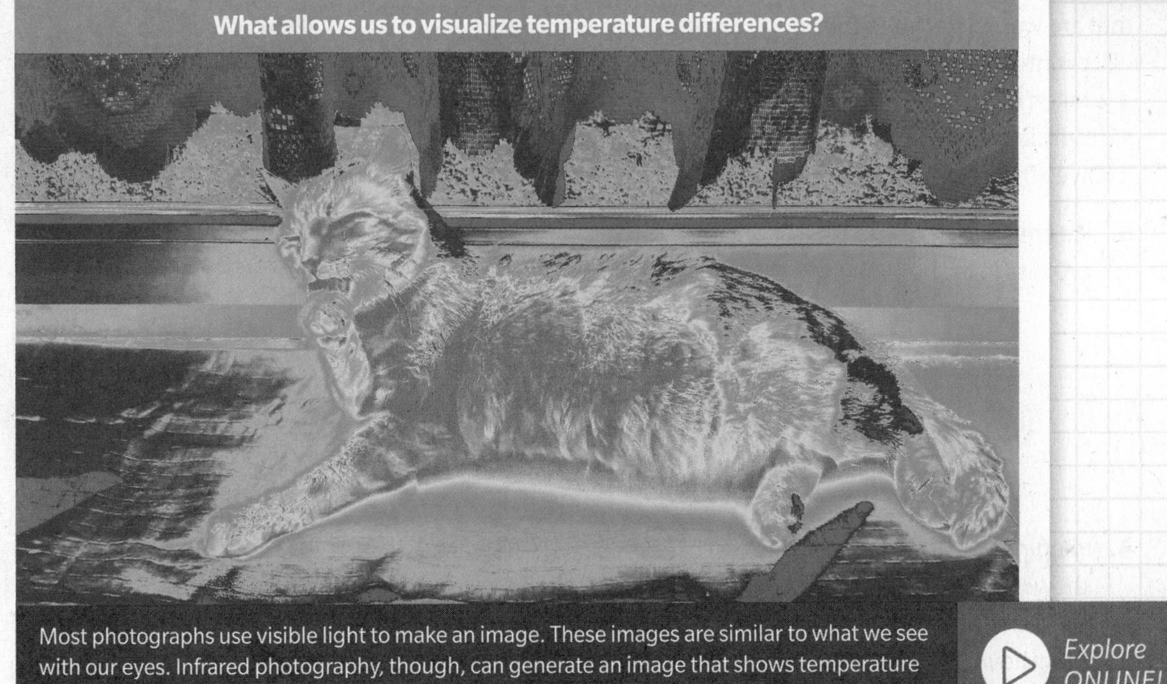

Most photographs use visible light to make an image. These images are similar to what we see with our eyes. Infrared photography, though, can generate an image that shows temperature differences. In this image, different colors indicate different temperatures.

Explore ONLINE!

1. What does it mean for objects to be at different temperatures? What is different about them physically?

2. Why do you think different temperatures appear as different colors on an infrared image?

EVIDENCE NOTEBOOK As you explore the lesson, gather evidence to help explain how temperature differences could be visualized.

Comparing Hot and Cold Objects

You come into contact with warm and cold objects every day. Objects that are warm relative to their surroundings do not stay that way. They will eventually cool. For example, hot soup begins to cool as soon as it is taken off the stove burner. Objects that are cold relative to their surroundings will warm. An ice cube starts to warm and melt as soon as it leaves the freezer.

As the ice cream warms, its particles have more kinetic energy.

3. Ice cream melts if you leave it out on a warm day. Describe this process in terms of energy and temperature.

4. Imagine you are holding an ice cream cone. Draw a diagram that shows how your hand, the ice cream cone, and the air around your hand and the ice cream cone are warming or cooling. Use arrows to show how energy is being transferred from one object or substance to another.

The Direction of Energy Transfer

If a hot pan is placed on a cool counter, the pan will warm both the countertop and the surrounding air. As the pan warms the countertop and air, the pan cools. This process continues until the pan, the air, and the countertop are all the same temperature. Similarly, if a cold pack is placed on your forehead, your forehead will cool and the cold pack will warm until they are the same temperature. When objects are at different temperatures, energy is transferred from the warmer object to the cooler object. This energy transfer can be modeled by using arrows to show how energy is flowing from warmer objects to cooler objects.

5. When two objects at different temperatures are in contact, thermal energy flows from the cooler / warmer object into the cooler / warmer object until the temperatures increase / are the same in both objects.

A hot pan on a countertop will transfer energy to the countertop and to the air around it until the pan, the countertop, and the air are all the same temperature.

Hot and Cold

When you touch an object and it feels warm, it is because energy is being transferred from that object to you. When an object feels cold, energy is being transferred from you to the object. Because energy flows from warmer objects to cooler objects, an object will usually feel warm to the touch if it is at a higher temperature than your hand. And if an object is at a lower temperature than your hand, it usually feels cool to the touch.

6. If you hold a glass of cold water, your hand will become cold. Describe how energy flows in this situation.

Energy is transferred from the hot liquid to the spoon and then from the hot spoon to your hand. This energy transfer causes the spoon to feel warm relative to your hand.

Analyze the Loss of Thermal Energy

7. Recall the photo of the melting ice cream. If you put the melted ice cream back into the freezer, it will become solid again. Describe the transfer of thermal energy as the ice cream melts and as it becomes solid again. In both situations, describe which objects are gaining and losing energy.

Relating Temperature and Thermal Energy

Suppose that you have two similar rocks in front of you. One rock has been sitting in the shade, and the other has been sitting in the sunlight. The two rocks look the same, but if you touch them, you will observe a difference. One rock will feel cold and the other rock will feel warm because the temperatures of the rocks are different. When you touch the rocks, you will know right away which one was in the sunlight.

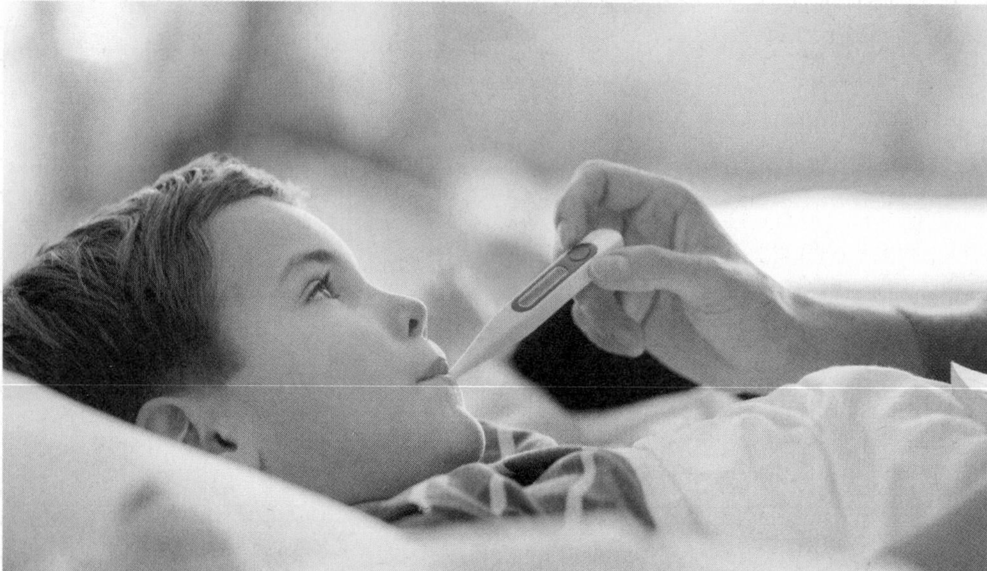

Thermometers are instruments that measure temperature.

8. What do you think the numbers on a thermometer actually mean? What physical property is a thermometer measuring?

Temperature

Think back to the hot and cold rocks. What makes one rock hot and the other cold? Like all matter, the rocks are made up of particles that are too small to be seen. These particles are in constant motion. Like all objects in motion, these particles have energy. The energy associated with their motion is kinetic energy. The faster the particles move, the greater their kinetic energy is.

Now think about the two rocks again. The particles of the warmer rock are moving faster than the particles of the cooler rock. Therefore, the warmer rock has more kinetic energy. **Temperature** is a measure of the *average* kinetic energy of all the particles in an object or substance. Temperature does not depend on the material or the type of particles in a substance.

Measure Temperature with Analog and Digital Thermometers

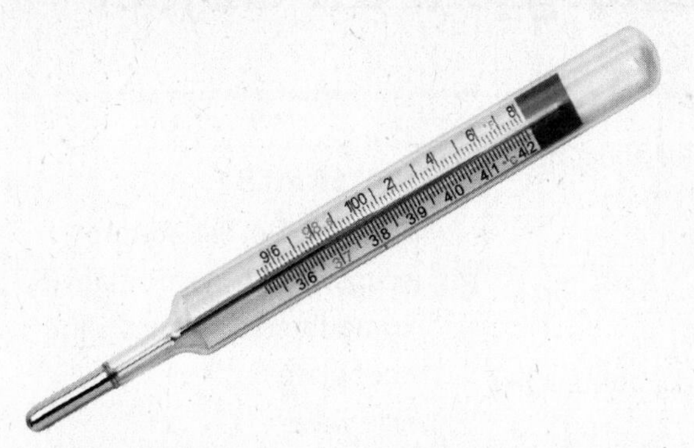

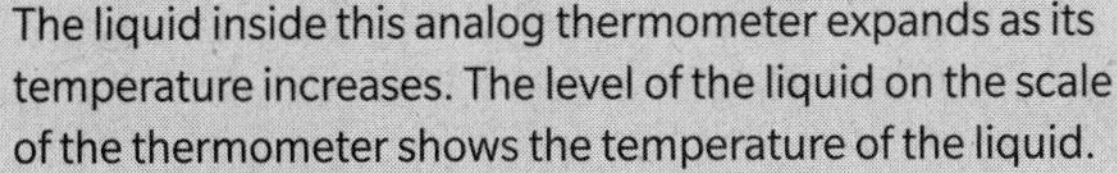

The liquid inside this analog thermometer expands as its temperature increases. The level of the liquid on the scale of the thermometer shows the temperature of the liquid.

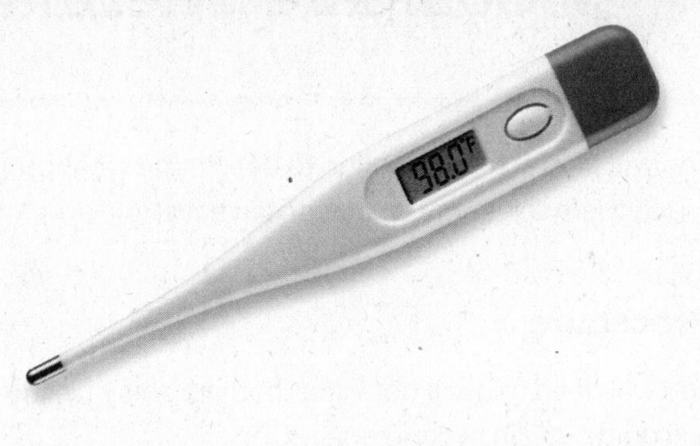

A digital thermometer measures the temperature of the tip of its probe. The digital thermometer displays this temperature as a number.

9. How is the size of an object related to its temperature measured by a thermometer?

- **A.** Larger objects have a higher temperature because they have more particles.
- **B.** Larger objects have a lower temperature because each particle has a smaller amount of energy.
- **C.** The size of an object does not affect temperature. Temperature is a measurement of average kinetic energy of all of the object's particles.
- **D.** The size of the object does not affect temperature because temperature is a measurement of the object's total kinetic energy.

Thermal Energy

Temperature is a measure of the average kinetic energy of an object. **Thermal energy** is the measurement of the total amount of kinetic energy of all the particles in an object or substance. Thermal energy is measured in joules (J). All matter has thermal energy. When an object is hot, its particles are moving faster and it has more thermal energy than it has when it is cold.

A quarter and a dime are made of the same materials. If the two coins have the same temperature, the quarter has more thermal energy than the dime. Although the average kinetic energy of their particles is the same, the quarter has many more particles than the dime, so the quarter has more total thermal energy.

If you warmed the dime until it melted, the melted dime would have more thermal energy than the solid dime had. This is because the particles in the melted dime are moving faster than the solid particles were. So the particles of the melted dime have more kinetic energy. Consider a glass of ice water in which the water and ice are both at the same temperature. The liquid water has more thermal energy than an equal mass of ice, even though they are at the same temperature. Liquid particles move much faster and have more energy than solid particles. Similarly, the particles in a gas have more energy than the particles in the liquid phase of the same substance.

Different kinds of matter are made up of different kinds of particles that do not interact with one another in the same way in each substance. Because of these differences, the amount of thermal energy in two different substances with equal mass can be different even if they have the same temperature.

Hands-On Lab

Compare Thermal Energy in an Object

You will plan an investigation to determine what properties affect how much thermal energy an object can have.

MATERIALS

- bowl, wide, flat bottom
- cups, small, plastic foam (5)
- graduated cylinder, 25 mL
- hot plate
- ice water
- thermometers, non-mercury (6)
- tongs
- washers, aluminum, 10 g
- washers, aluminum, 20 g
- water
- weight, brass, 20 g
- weight, rubber, 10 g

Procedure

You will need to use a hot water bath for this investigation. Your teacher will guide you in making one.

As you develop your plan, consider these questions:

- How can you indirectly determine the thermal energy of the objects? (Hint: Think about how a hot object would affect water if placed in the water.)
- What data should you measure and record?
- Which objects will you test to provide data to answer your questions?

STEP 1 Plan and write your procedure to determine the properties that affect the amount of thermal energy an object can contain. Your procedure should describe how to test the amount of thermal energy four different objects have.

STEP 2 Get your teacher's approval before you begin your investigation. Make any changes to your procedure requested by your teacher.

STEP 3 Perform your investigation, following the steps you have written. Record your observations on a separate sheet of paper.

STEP 4 Rank the objects by the amount of thermal energy they seemed to contain.

1. ______________________________

2. ______________________________

3. ______________________________

4. ______________________________

STEP 5 Which factors seem to affect the amount of thermal energy an object has? Select all that apply.

A. mass

B. shape

C. color

D. material

STEP 6 **Language SmArts** If time allows, trade procedures with another group and follow the steps that they used. Did you get the same results? Why or why not?

Factors Affecting the Thermal Energy in an Object

Every object has thermal energy because every object's particles are moving. In the Hands-On Lab, when you placed a hot object in cold water, the temperature of the water increased. The change in water temperature was not the same for all of the objects. The object with the larger mass had more energy than the smaller object of the same material at the same temperature. Because it had more energy, the larger object warmed the water to a higher temperature after a certain amount of time.

The brass and aluminum objects that had the same mass warmed the water by different amounts, so this is evidence that the thermal energy of an object also depends on the material it is made of. Different materials of the same size and same temperature can have different amounts of thermal energy.

EVIDENCE NOTEBOOK

10. The infrared photograph indicates that the surfaces and air nearer the cat are warmer than the surfaces and air farther away. What factors might cause these temperature differences? Record your evidence.

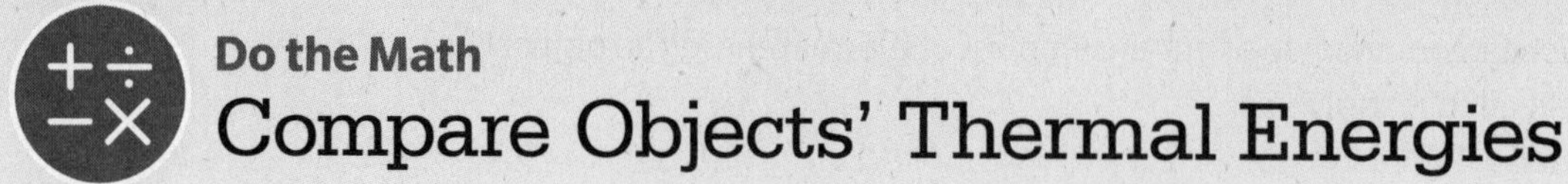

Do the Math

Compare Objects' Thermal Energies

All matter has some amount of thermal energy—even the coldest object you have ever felt. But the actual amount of thermal energy varies among objects of different temperatures and of different materials. The thermal energy in any object is related to its mass, its composition, its state, and its temperature.

11. Look at the photos of the two rocks and the information in the caption. Think about how the rocks are different. Which rock has a greater amount of thermal energy? Explain your answer.

These two rocks are made of the same substance and are the same temperature, but have different masses. The rock on the right has significantly less mass than the rock on the left.

12. Place these objects in order by the amount of thermal energy they contain. Number the boxes so that they are ordered from least thermal energy (1) to greatest thermal energy (5). Assume that the iceberg and the lake have similar masses.

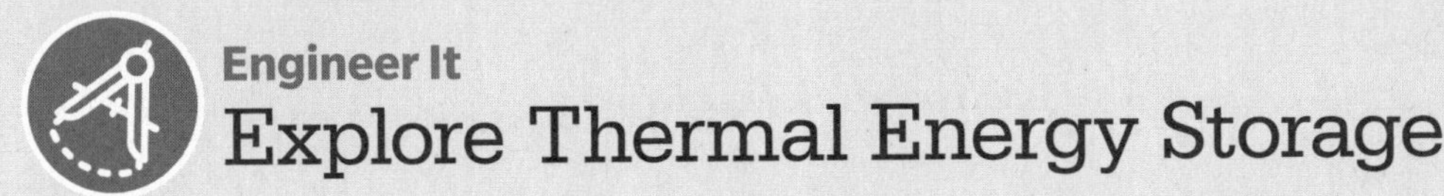

Engineer It

Explore Thermal Energy Storage

Solar energy systems do not produce energy at a constant rate. Sometimes, they generate more electrical energy than people need. At other times, they do not generate any energy. A thermal battery is one way to store the extra energy for use later. When the sun is shining, the system adds thermal energy to a solid, such as salt. As the thermal energy of the salt increases, it melts. The energy stored in the molten material is later used to warm other objects or produce an electric current.

This giant mirror focuses sunlight onto material in the box.

13. Some solar power plants use mirrors to focus sunlight on a central collector. The energy from sunlight causes water in the central collector to boil and produce steam. A generator uses the kinetic energy of the steam to produce electricity. How could a molten salt battery help this type of power plant generate electricity 24 hours per day?

EVIDENCE NOTEBOOK

14. If two objects have the same temperatures, will they always have the same thermal energies? Record your evidence.

Analyzing Heat

Suppose that you are standing outside on a sunny day. The skin on your arms feels very warm in the sunlight. Suddenly a cloud comes between you and the sun. A thermometer would show that the temperature of the air near you has not changed very much. Your skin feels much cooler, though. As the cloud moves away, you start to feel warmer.

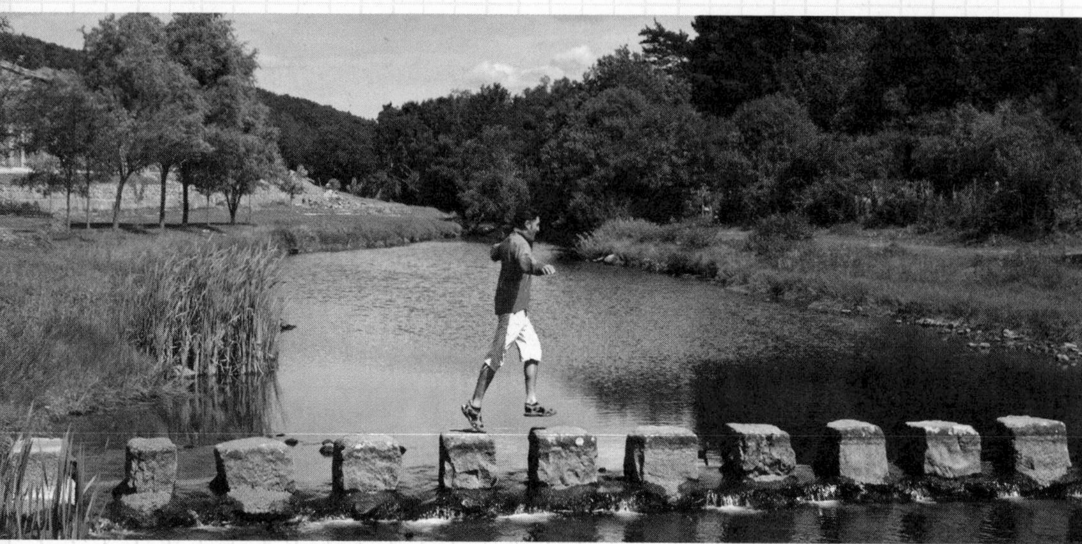

A sunny place usually feels warmer than a shady place even if a thermometer shows little to no temperature difference in the air.

15. Why might you feel warmer in a sunny place than in a shady place, even though the air temperature is the same?

Heat

Think about what happens when you boil water on the stove. The pot of water becomes warmer while it is over the stove. This is because thermal energy is being transferred to the water. Energy flows from the stove to the pot of water as heat. You may have heard *heat* used in other ways in everyday language, but in science, heat has a specific definition. **Heat** is the energy that is transferred between two objects that are at different temperatures.

When thermal energy is transferred to an object as heat, the average kinetic energy of the particles of the object will increase. And so the temperature of the object will rise. Heat always flows from an object at a higher temperature to an object at a lower temperature. Heat will flow as long as there is a temperature difference. If no energy is added to the system, both objects will eventually have the same temperature.

It is sometimes helpful to know how much thermal energy transfer is needed to change the temperature of a substance by a certain amount. For example, a materials scientist might want to know how much energy it would take to melt a metal sample. The amount of thermal energy transfer needed to change the temperature of a substance depends on the identity of the substance, the size, or mass, of the sample, and the system surrounding the substance.

Conduction, Convection, and Radiation

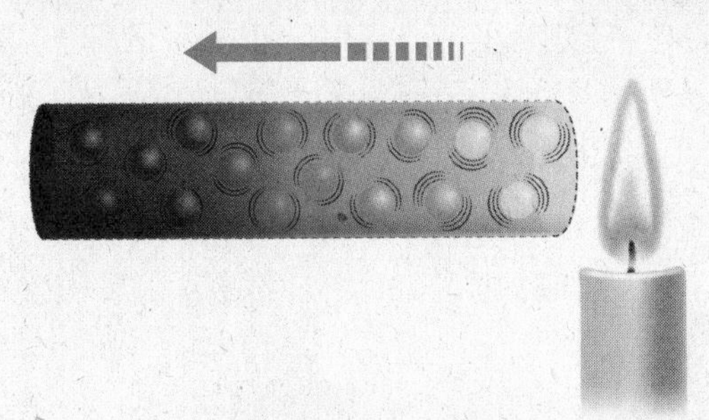

Conduction Thermal energy is transferred between particles through conduction. In this example, the candle is warming one end of the metal bar. The particles in the metal bar start to move faster as they gain more thermal energy. As the particles move faster, they bump into each other and transfer thermal energy through the metal rod.

Convection Thermal energy is transferred throughout liquids and gases through convection. In this example, the candle is heating the box. As air in the box warms, the air particles begin to move faster and the air becomes less dense. The colder, denser air sinks and pushes up the warmer air. This movement transfers thermal energy through liquids and gases.

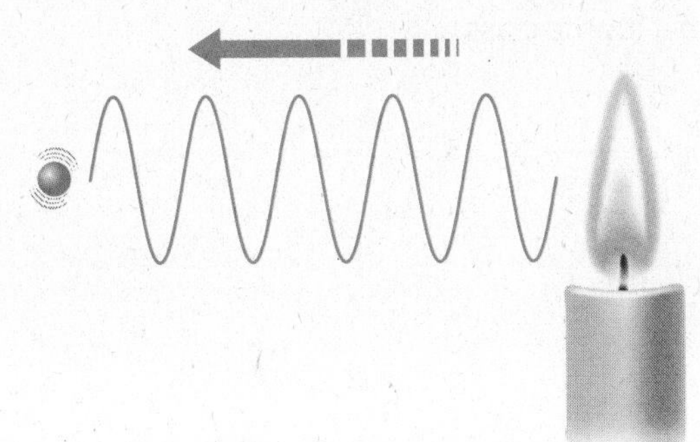

Radiation Radiation is the transfer of energy through electromagnetic waves. In this example, the candle produces infrared radiation. This radiation travels through empty space until it hits a particle. The particle then absorbs this radiation, and the radiation is converted into thermal energy. This process is how thermal energy is transferred through space.

Three Types of Energy Transfer

To remove a metal pan from a hot oven, you must use an insulated pad or glove. If you do not, energy will transfer quickly to your hand by conduction. The pan is much hotter than your skin, so its particles have a lot more thermal energy. When the metal's particles bump into the particles of your skin, energy is transferred.

If the hot pan is on top of the stove, you can tell that it is hot by holding your hand above the pan. The moving air around the pan absorbs energy and carries it to your skin by convection. You can also absorb energy by holding your hand to the side of a stove's heating element. Energy is transferred through radiation from the fire to your skin.

Energy in the form of heat can be transferred by conduction, convection, and radiation. During all three types of energy transfer, the thermal energy of the warmer object decreases and the thermal energy of the cooler object increases. In all three types of energy transfer, energy is being transferred to a cooler object.

EVIDENCE NOTEBOOK

16. Infrared photography produces images showing the temperature ranges of different objects. What type of energy transfer is necessary for infrared photography? Explain your answer.

17. Which types of energy transfer might occur in a solar oven as it cooks a bowl of soup? Explain how each of the three types of energy transfer occurs in the oven as the soup is cooked.

Radiation carries energy from the sun. By using a solar oven, this energy is directed at a single object to cook food.

18. Act With your group, plan a short skit in which you model what occurs when energy is transferred between objects by one of the three methods of thermal energy transfer. Focus on making your performance convey information as accurately as possible. Record the plan for your skit and then perform it for the class.

Compare Thermal Conductivities

Different substances can absorb or transfer energy at different rates. For example, cooks often prefer a wooden spoon to a metal spoon for stirring a hot liquid. This is because a spoon made of wood absorbs energy slowly and will not get very hot. A metal spoon will absorb energy quickly and become too hot to hold. Thermal conductivity is a property of matter that refers to how quickly a material transfers and absorbs energy as heat.

19. Suppose that you are an engineer who is designing a heat exchanger to remove energy from a motor rapidly. Energy will be transferred from the motor to the heat exchanger. Then the energy will be transferred from the heat exchanger to the air. The table shows the thermal conductivities of a few substances as measured in W/m•K. The greater the thermal conductivity, the faster the rate of energy transfer. Which material would be the best choice?

A. copper

B. glass

C. polystyrene

D. steel

Substance	Thermal conductivity (W/m·K)
Copper	385
Glass	0.8
Polystyrene	0.033
Steel	50

Continue Your Exploration

Name: Date:

Check out the path below or go online to choose one of the other paths shown.

Heat and Cooking

- Hands-On Labs
- Heat and Computing
- Propose Your Own Path

Go online to choose one of these other paths.

A good cook must understand temperature, thermal energy, and heat. The energy added to food during cooking causes chemical changes in the substances that make up the food. It is important to control the amount of energy absorbed by the food. Too much energy, and the food will be overcooked. Too little energy, and food will still be raw. It is also important to control the rate of energy transfer. If energy is added too quickly or too slowly, the food may have the wrong texture or it might cook unevenly.

1. How might using a pizza stone instead of a pan affect how the pizza cooks?
   A. The stone gets hotter than the rest of the oven, so the pizza cooks faster.
   B. The stone transfers energy slowly, so the crust cooks evenly.
   C. The stone absorbs energy, keeping the crust cooler than the pizza toppings.

2. Pizza restaurants often use large ovens lined with bricks. These ovens remain very hot, even though only a small fire is kept burning in the oven. Why might this be?

Pizzas can be cooked in an oven using a pizza stone, a pizza pan, or no pan at all. The pizza stone absorbs and releases energy more slowly than a pizza pan does.

Continue Your Exploration

If food is cooked too quickly, the outside can burn, while the inside of the food is still raw.

3. What might cause the food to not cook all the way through?

A. Not enough energy reaches the center of the food.

B. Energy flows into the food too quickly and is lost before the inside is cooked.

C. The food conducts energy, so the energy passes through the food without cooking it.

D. The energy cooks the outside of the food, and then the food begins to lose heat instead of cooking further.

4. If the oven is too hot, the bottom part of cookies on a metal tray can become hard and black. Why would the bottom of the cookies burn first?

5. Collaborate With a partner, research one or more recipes. Make a presentation that shows how the method of cooking described in the recipe or recipes affects the food.

Can You Explain It?

Name: ______________________ Date: ______________________

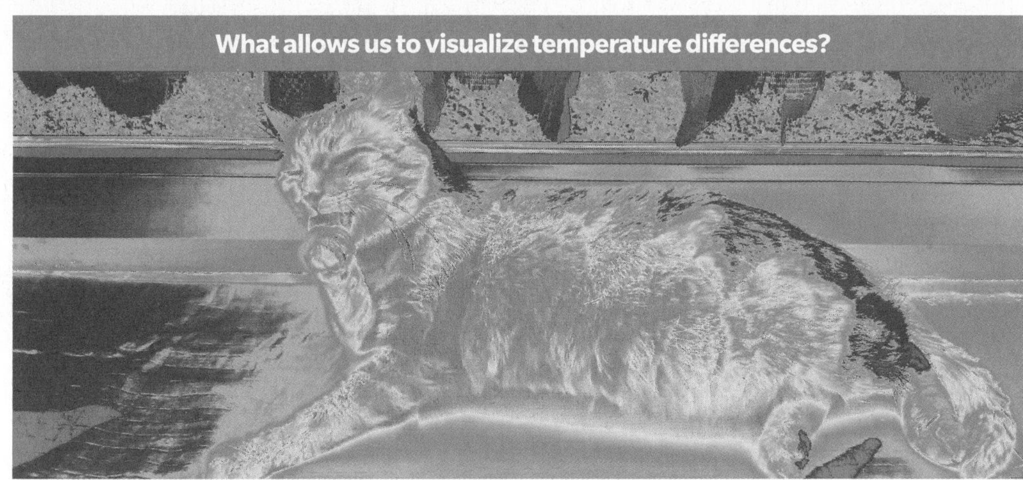
What allows us to visualize temperature differences?

Explore ONLINE!

EVIDENCE NOTEBOOK

Refer to the notes in your Evidence Notebook to help you construct an explanation for how infrared photography can be used to visualize temperature differences.

1. State your claim. Make sure your claim fully explains how infrared photography can be used to visualize temperature differences.

2. Summarize the evidence you have gathered to support your claim and explain your reasoning.

Checkpoints

Answer the following questions to check your understanding of the lesson.

Use the photograph to answer Question 3.

3. Energy flows through a system that consists of the stove, the pan, the boiling water, and the air around these objects. Which of the following statements describe a direction that energy is moving in this system? Select all that apply.

   A. the stove to the pan

   B. the pan to the water

   C. the water to the pan

   D. the pan to the stove

---

4. Suppose you had a glass that was partially filled with water. Which of the following statements describe ways that you could raise the thermal energy of the glass of water? Select all that apply.

   A. Remove water from the glass.

   B. Add water of the same temperature to the glass.

   C. Warm the glass of water using a microwave.

   D. Cool the glass of water using a refrigerator.

Use the photo and table to answer Questions 5–6.

5. On a sunny day, the sidewalk and the street are both warmer than the atmosphere because they have more heat / thermal energy due to energy transfer by conduction / radiation from the sun.

6. A student used a thermometer to measure the temperature at three places and recorded the data in a table. Which statements represent conclusions that you can support with these data? Select all that apply.

   A. The temperature of the sidewalk is the same as the temperature of the street.

   B. Energy has been transferred from the street to the air above the street.

   C. Energy has been transferred from the lawn to the street and the sidewalk through conduction.

   D. The street surface has absorbed more radiant thermal energy than the sidewalk.

Location	Temperature
0.5 m above street	38 °C
0.5 m above sidewalk	33 °C
0.5 m above grass lawn	27 °C

Interactive Review

Complete this section to review the main concepts of the lesson.

Humans perceive objects as hot or cold due to temperature differences and the transfer of energy.

A. Recall a situation when you felt a hot or cold object. Discuss the temperature differences involved and the direction in which the energy was being transferred.

Thermal energy is the total kinetic energy of the particles that make up a substance. Temperature is a measure of the average kinetic energy of the particles that make up a substance.

B. Describe how an object's thermal energy will change and how the particles in the object will be affected when the object's temperature increases.

Heat is the energy transferred between two objects that are at different temperatures. Energy in the form of heat can be transferred by conduction, convection, or radiation.

C. Describe situations in which energy is transferred through conduction, convection, and radiation.

Thermal Energy Transfer in Systems

Used, or *spent*, nuclear fuel rods are stored at the bottom of a cooling pool at the nuclear power plant in Chinon, France.

By the end of this lesson . . .

you will be able to explain how thermal energy is transferred and use this knowledge to design a device to minimize thermal energy transfer.

Go online to view the digital version of the Hands-On Lab for this lesson and to download additional lab resources.

CAN YOU EXPLAIN IT?

Why are urban heat islands hotter than their surrounding regions?

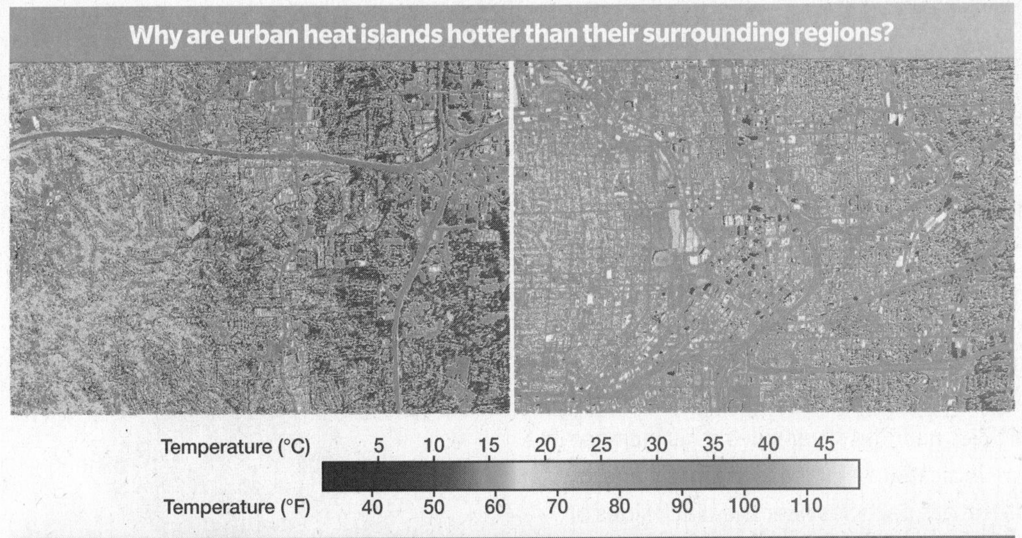

These satellite images of suburban (left) and urban (right) Atlanta, Georgia, show the differences in daytime temperatures in the region. The images show the two areas at the same time and on the same day.

Using a variety of tools ranging from thermometers to satellite images, scientists have collected data about the average temperature in many places. The data show that urban areas are often significantly warmer than the rural places nearby. These warmer areas inside cities are called *urban heat islands*.

1. Think about how surfaces in cities differ from those in the surrounding areas. Why might a central city contain more thermal energy than a farm or forest?

2. What might be some negative consequences of the increased temperatures within an urban heat island?

EVIDENCE NOTEBOOK As you explore the lesson, gather evidence to help explain the causes of urban heat islands.

Modeling the Flow of Thermal Energy through Systems

Energy Transfer

A radiometer, or light-mill, is a device that responds to light. When the radiometer is exposed to a bright light source, the vanes of the radiometer rotate. Why does the radiometer spin when it is placed in a bright source of light?

The vanes of the radiometer are black on one side and silver on the other. The black surfaces absorb more energy from the light than the silver surfaces, so they become warmer. The gas particles near the black sides of the vanes warm up more than the gas particles near the silver sides. This increase in temperature indicates an increase in kinetic energy. This means the gas particles near the black sides of the vanes collide with the vanes more frequently and with more energy than the cooler gas particles on the silver sides do. The transfer of energy from the collisions causes the vanes of the radiometer to spin.

The vanes of a radiometer spin when they are exposed to bright light.

3. What is the energy input to the radiometer system? What form(s) of energy are present in the system as a result?

A transfer of energy results in a change in the energy in an object when energy is added to it or removed from it. You can think of the entire radiometer as a **system**, or a set of interacting parts that work together. The vanes of the radiometer move because of a transfer of electromagnetic energy from a light source into the radiometer system.

The law of conservation of energy states that energy cannot be created or destroyed. The total energy of a system will increase if the input of energy from outside the system is greater than its output. By defining a system's boundaries, the inputs and outputs of energy can be modeled. The bulb is the boundary of the radiometer system. When the radiometer is exposed to a bright light source, the input of electromagnetic energy will be greater than the loss of thermal energy from the system.

EVIDENCE NOTEBOOK

4. Think about the energy inputs and outputs in an urban area. How do urban heat islands demonstrate the law of conservation of energy?

The Flow of Thermal Energy

Thermal energy is the kinetic energy of the particles in an object. This energy can flow as heat between parts of a system. Thermal energy is transferred three ways. Thermal energy is transferred by *conduction* when particles collide. *Convection* describes the transfer of thermal energy through the motion of particles of a fluid. In *radiation*, energy is transferred when electromagnetic waves are emitted by a warmer object and absorbed by a cooler object. Thermal energy always flows from components of a system at higher temperatures to components at lower temperatures.

Models of Thermal Energy Transfer in Systems

During the operation of a nuclear reactor, fuel rods in the reactor core produce a large amount of thermal energy. This energy is used to generate electrical energy. This energy is transferred to homes, schools, and businesses. After the used fuel rods are removed from a nuclear reactor, they are still very hot. These hot fuel rods are stored in cooling pools filled with water. Thermal energy from the hot fuel rods is transferred to the cooler water. As the fuel rods cool down, the temperature of the water in the pool increases. The rods eventually cool to just above the temperature of the warming water in the pool. Because the rods continue to produce thermal energy, they will always be a little warmer than the water.

Nuclear Cooling Pool

The used fuel rods from a nuclear reactor are stored in cooling pools, where thermal energy is transferred from the hot fuel rods to the cool water.

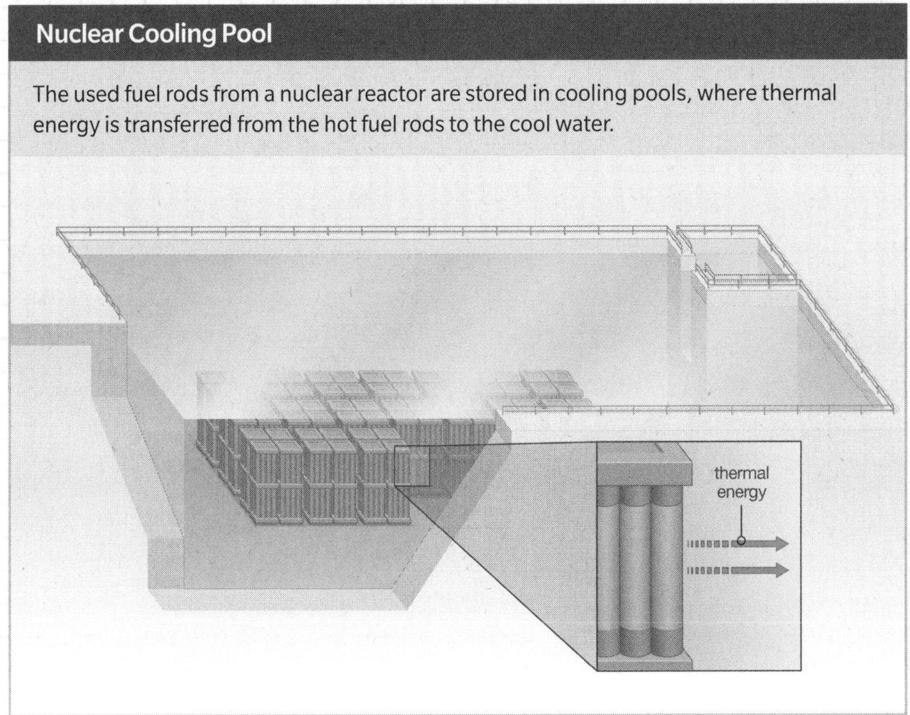

5. How would the temperatures of the components of this system change if additional hot fuel rods were placed in the pool after a steady temperature was reached?

A. The temperature of the water and the original fuel rods would decrease.

B. The temperature of the water and the original fuel rods would increase.

C. The temperature of the water would decrease but the temperature of the original fuel rods would not change.

D. The temperature of the water would increase but the temperature of the original fuel rods would not change.

Thermal Energy Transfer and Ambient Temperature

All parts of a system will eventually reach the same temperature if there are no inputs or outputs of energy. The temperature of an object's surroundings is called the *ambient temperature*. For example, a building is a system surrounded by the ambient outdoor environment. If thermal energy is not added to the building, the indoor temperature will eventually become the same as the ambient outdoor temperature. If you light a fire in a fireplace, the building will become warmer than the ambient outdoor temperature.

Without energy inputs, the buildings will cool down to the ambient temperature.

6. Think of a window in a house as a system boundary separating the air on opposite sides of the glass pane. Diagram the flow of thermal energy through the window when the indoor temperature is 23 °C and the outdoor temperature is 15 °C. Then show how the system model would change if the temperature outside were warmer than inside. How would bright sunshine affect the system?

Analyze Solar Heaters

Hot water from the faucets in your school is warmer than water that comes into the building from the water supply. Most water heaters use a combustible fuel, such as natural gas, or electrical energy to raise the water temperature. Solar water heaters raise the temperature of water by converting electromagnetic energy from the sun into thermal energy. These water heaters are generally placed on the roof of the building. After it is warmed, water flows to a hot water tank inside the building.

These solar water heaters convert electromagnetic energy into thermal energy.

7. Sometimes, the hot water produced by a solar water heater is not warm enough to meet the needs of the occupants of a building. A traditional water heater inside the building supplies additional thermal energy to the solar-warmed water. How can this method still reduce the overall amount of natural gas or electricity a building uses?

Describing the Thermal Properties of Materials

Pastry chefs around the world bake pies in plates with a similar shape, but they disagree on the best material for the plates. Some bakers claim they get the best results from shiny aluminum plates. Some chefs never use any material other than glass. A third group argues that ceramic is definitely the way to go.

8. Why might the material of a pie plate have an effect on the quality of the pie's crust?

A common problem when baking pies is burnt crust.

The Thermal Energy of an Object

The thermal energy of an object is the total kinetic energy of its particles. An object's thermal energy depends on the mass of the object, its temperature, its state of matter, and its chemical composition. Larger objects have more thermal energy than smaller objects of the same material at the same temperature. A liquid substance has more thermal energy than the same mass of the substance in its solid form.

9. Suppose you have two identical objects made of the same mass of the same material. If one object is 20 °C warmer than the other, which object has more thermal energy?

10. Suppose you have two similar objects made of the same material but with different masses. If both objects are the same temperature, which object has more thermal energy?

The amount of thermal energy an object has increases as its temperature increases because its particles are moving faster. A greater mass of the same substance at the same temperature will also contain more thermal energy. This is because it contains more moving particles. The composition of the object also affects the thermal energy because some materials are more likely to absorb thermal energy than others. Thermal energy is also related to a material's physical state, or phase. When a solid reaches its melting point or a liquid reaches its boiling point, its physical state changes.

Hands-On Lab

Examine the Transfer of Thermal Energy through Radiation

In this activity, you will investigate how the composition of an object affects its absorption of thermal energy through radiation.

MATERIALS

- adjustable desk lamps, each with at least 60 watt incandescent light bulbs (2)
- graduated cylinder, 100 mL
- plastic foam disks that can fit onto the tops of cans, each with a hole in the middle for a thermometer (2)
- ruler
- stopwatch or timer
- thermometers (2)
- tin cans of the same size (2), one painted matte black and the other painted matte white
- water

Procedure and Analysis

STEP 1 Use a graduated cylinder to measure and pour the same amount of water into each of the two cans. The cans should be almost full.

STEP 2 Place a plastic foam cover on each can and insert a thermometer through the hole in the cover. Measure the temperature of the water in each can and record the value at time zero in the data table. The water in both cans should be approximately the same temperature.

STEP 3 Use the ruler to place each lamp the same distance from both cans. Turn on both lamps at the same time and begin timing the experiment.

STEP 4 Record the temperature of the water in both cans every 5 minutes for 30 minutes. On a separate piece of paper, graph your data showing the temperature of the water in each can over time.

STEP 5 Describe your observations about each can's absorption of radiation. Why does the water in the two cans have different temperatures at the end of the experiment?

	Temperature (°C)	
Time (min)	White can	Black can
0		
5		
10		
15		
20		
25		
30		

EVIDENCE NOTEBOOK

11. How could paving roads with concrete or other light-colored materials instead of dark-colored asphalt affect urban heat islands?

Changes in Thermal Energy

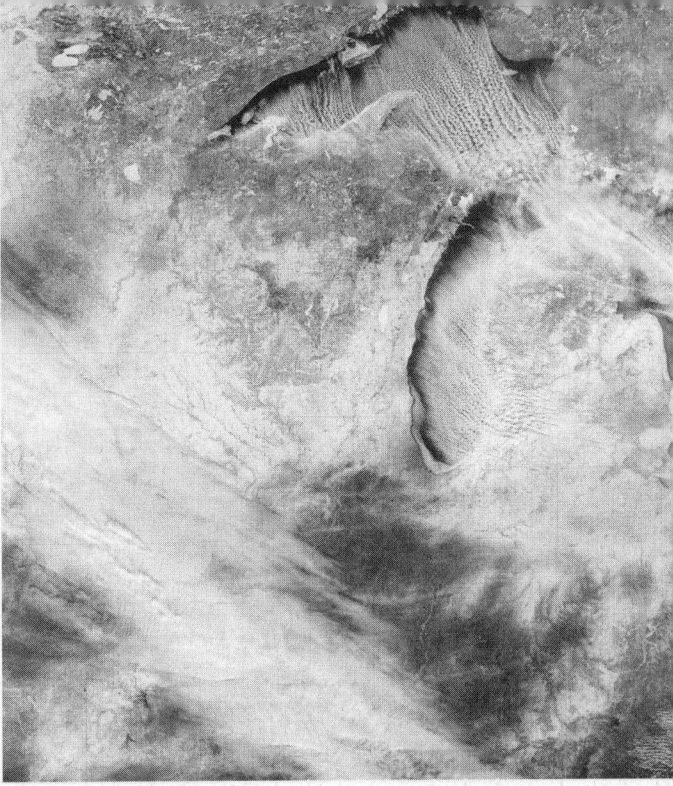

This satellite image shows bands of lake-effect snow forming along the shores of Lake Superior and Lake Michigan as moist air from over the lakes cools above colder land.

The total thermal energy of a particular component of a system depends on its temperature, mass, composition, and physical state. Different parts of a system can have different temperatures. Differences in thermal energy and temperature affect the transfer of energy to and from the system, as well as within the system. For example, water is able to absorb more thermal energy than the same amount of soil or rock. For this reason, the temperature of land near large bodies of water is influenced by the temperature of the water. A large lake will change temperature more slowly than the surrounding land. In winter, as cold air moves through, the land around the shore of the lake will remain warmer than areas farther inland. This "lake effect" causes many areas close to the shore of a lake to have much more snow than areas a few kilometers away. As air moves over the lake, the lower layer of air is warmed. This warmer air carries more water vapor from the lake. As this air again cools while passing over colder land, the water vapor precipitates to form snow.

12. Different materials absorb and release thermal energy at different rates. How might you use this property to control the temperatures of components within a system?

The Thermal Properties of Substances

Think about baking something in a hot oven. When you take the pan out of the oven, you use a padded cloth potholder to hold the hot dish. Could you use a sheet of aluminum foil as a potholder? That would not be a good idea. It is likely that you would burn your hands. How an object absorbs and transfers thermal energy depends on the materials from which it is made. Some substances transfer thermal energy better than others. Aluminum foil rapidly transfers thermal energy from the pan to your hand. The cloth potholder does not.

You can also also observe how different materials absorb and transfer thermal energy by considering a bicycle sitting in the sun on a hot summer day. The metal frame of the bike feels much hotter than the plastic handlebar grips. Metals, such as aluminum or steel, transfer thermal energy to your hand much faster than plastic. Engineers consider these differences in properties of materials during the design process. Because some materials conduct heat better than others, heat will flow differently depending on the materials used. The transfer of thermal energy to and from an object does not just depend on the difference between the temperatures of the object and its surroundings. It also depends on the material from which the object is made.

Differences in Thermal Energy Transfer

Does knowing that different materials have different properties of thermal energy transfer help solve the pie-plate debate? Aluminum, glass, and ceramic each transfer thermal energy differently. The table shows the thermal conductivity values for these materials. Thermal conductivity is a measure of how quickly a material transfers thermal energy, measured in watts per meter-kelvin (W/m•K). The higher the value, the faster the material transfers energy.

The values in the table indicate that an aluminum pie plate will conduct heat much more quickly than a glass or ceramic plate. This means that thermal energy will transfer to the pie crust through conduction faster in an aluminum plate. A glass pie plate will conduct heat much more slowly. Because glass is clear, the transfer of radiant thermal energy will be greater in the glass plate. Even though ceramic has a higher thermal conductivity value, a ceramic plate is likely to cook the crust more slowly than a glass plate. It does not transfer thermal energy by radiation.

Thermal Conductivities of Substances

Substance	Thermal conductivity (W/m•K)
Aluminum	205
Ceramic	1.5
Glass	1.1
Stainless steel	16

13. Discuss Based on the thermal properties of aluminum, glass, and ceramic, how would you revise your recommendation for a pie-plate material? Would one material be preferable to the others based on the pie you are baking?

Engineer It

Analyze Evaporative Cooling

The thermal energy of a substance is related to its physical state. The particles of a gas move faster than those of a liquid, so the gas carries more thermal energy. In dry climates, people often use evaporative coolers instead of air conditioners. In an evaporative cooler, water changes from liquid to gas by absorbing some thermal energy from the hot, dry air as the air passes through a damp evaporative pad. As the air loses thermal energy to the water, it becomes cooler.

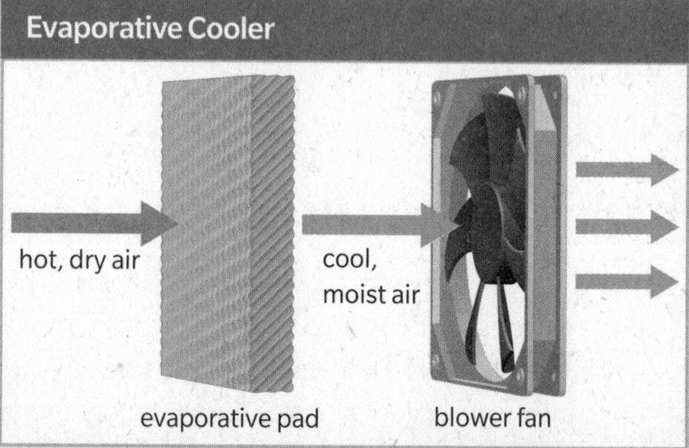

14. As plants grow, they release water vapor into the atmosphere around them. How can increasing the coverage of green rooftops in an urban area help to reduce the negative impact of an urban heat island?

This green roof on top of Chicago's City Hall saves the city approximately $5,000 a year in heating and cooling for the building and provides an urban garden space.

Applying the Concepts of Heat Transfer

The application of the transfer of thermal energy in real-world situations is often referred to as "heat transfer." Engineers and designers are often required to develop solutions to control heat transfer. For example, greenhouses are often designed to maximize the amount of radiant thermal energy taken in during sunny hours. They also minimize the amount of convective thermal energy lost to the atmosphere at night. One way to store thermal energy is to use a thermal mass. A thermal mass is a material that absorbs thermal energy when the air around it is warmer, and then slowly releases it when the air is cooler. Many greenhouses use big black barrels filled with water for this purpose. The barrels absorb thermal energy during the day and release thermal energy during the night.

In this greenhouse, the concrete floor acts as a thermal mass by absorbing radiant energy during the day and slowly releasing it after sundown.

Identify a Heat Transfer Problem: Design a Safe Lunch Carrier

People sometimes call a lunch that someone carries to work or school a "brown bag" lunch, but a paper bag is not always a safe way to carry food. Some foods do not have to be kept cold to be safe. However, lunches that include items such as meats, cheeses, milk, sliced fruits, or salads should stay cold. Bacteria that can make you sick grow quickly when the temperature of the food is between 4 °C and 60 °C. That means that the food carrier must keep chilled food almost as cold as a refrigerator at home. Hot food must stay above 60 °C to be safe.

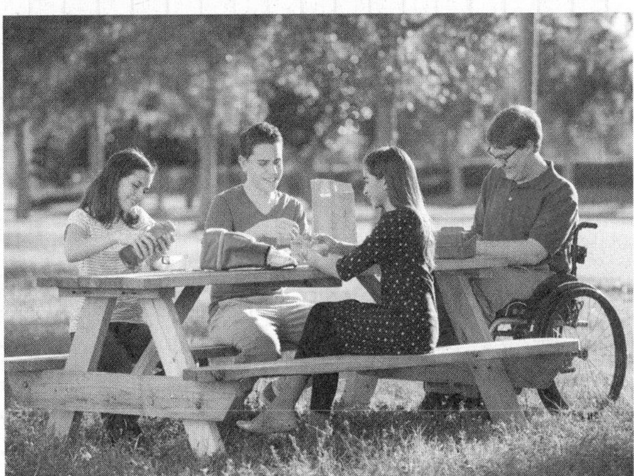

Insulated containers for hot and cold foods can help to keep packed lunches safe.

The engineering process begins with defining the engineering problem. In this case, the problem is to design a container that keeps chilled food at a safe temperature long enough to last until lunch.

The next step in the engineering design process is to precisely define the criteria and constraints of an acceptable solution. The criteria for the problem are the properties that the product must have in order to successfully solve the problem. Think about what the container has to do in order to solve the problem in this situation. Constraints are limitations on the solution. For example, a small refrigerator might meet the criterion of keeping food cold. It would not be a successful solution if there is a constraint that the container must be inexpensive.

Define the Criteria

Because this engineering problem involves heat transfer, an important criterion is whether the heat transfer should be maximized or minimized. In this case, the goal is to minimize heat transfer. You can begin defining the criteria for this engineering problem by stating that the solution should reduce heat transfer as much as possible. Another criterion might be to make sure that any heat transfer that does happen will occur slowly. A specific statement could be that the solution will hold a chilled lunch that starts at 2 °C for five hours at a temperature of 7 °C or below.

15. The goals of the design problem are not only to minimize heat transfer. Because this is a design for a carrier for taking lunch to school, you might want to consider other criteria, such as appearance and size. What are some criteria that you would include to define the problem more precisely?

16. Consider your list of criteria for a lunch carrier design. Think about the purpose of the designed product. Which criterion is the most important one you should consider when preparing a decision matrix to analyze possible solutions?

Define the Constraints

Along with its criteria, every engineering problem has constraints. Identifying the constraints helps you think about possible solutions more realistically. What kind of constraints might apply to a lunch carrier engineering problem? They might include the availability of materials, the amount of money that you have to spend, safety considerations, and environmental or societal impacts.

17. Discuss What are some of the constraints of the lunch container problem?

Design Heat Transfer Solutions

After you have clearly defined the problem and determined its criteria and constraints, you can begin to work on a solution. It is often helpful to brainstorm possible solutions based on background research. Before designing a safe lunch container, think about the thermal properties of different common materials you could use to construct a container. You have already identified minimizing heat transfer as an important criterion of the problem.

Do the Math

Compare Thermal Properties of Different Materials

Some materials transfer thermal energy very quickly. These materials are called *thermal conductors*. Other materials, known as *thermal insulators*, transfer energy slowly. The thermal conductivity values shown in this table compare how quickly the materials transfer heat. Recall that materials with higher thermal conductivity values transfer thermal energy more quickly than materials with lower thermal conductivity values.

Thermal Conductivities of Substances

Substance	Thermal conductivity (W/m•K)
Aluminum	205
Cloth (wool)	0.07
Copper	401
Polyethylene plastic	0.42
Polystyrene foam	0.03
Tin	67
Wood (pine)	0.12

18. Based on the data in the table above, which materials might work the best in designing a safe lunch container? Use evidence to explain your answer.

19. **Collaborate** With a group, use information from the text and your own experiences to brainstorm design solutions. Besides the thermal properties of the materials you use to build your lunch container, consider other design features that might be important for your solution. Record every suggestion made by your group members.

Choose the Best Solutions

After brainstorming, your group will have a number of ideas that can be used for solutions. Some of them will be more likely to solve the problem than others. Now evaluate and critique each possible solution. First, eliminate any solutions that violate the constraints of the problem. Next, compare how successfully the remaining solutions meet the criteria. Rate each solution based on the importance of criteria using a numerical score in a decision matrix.

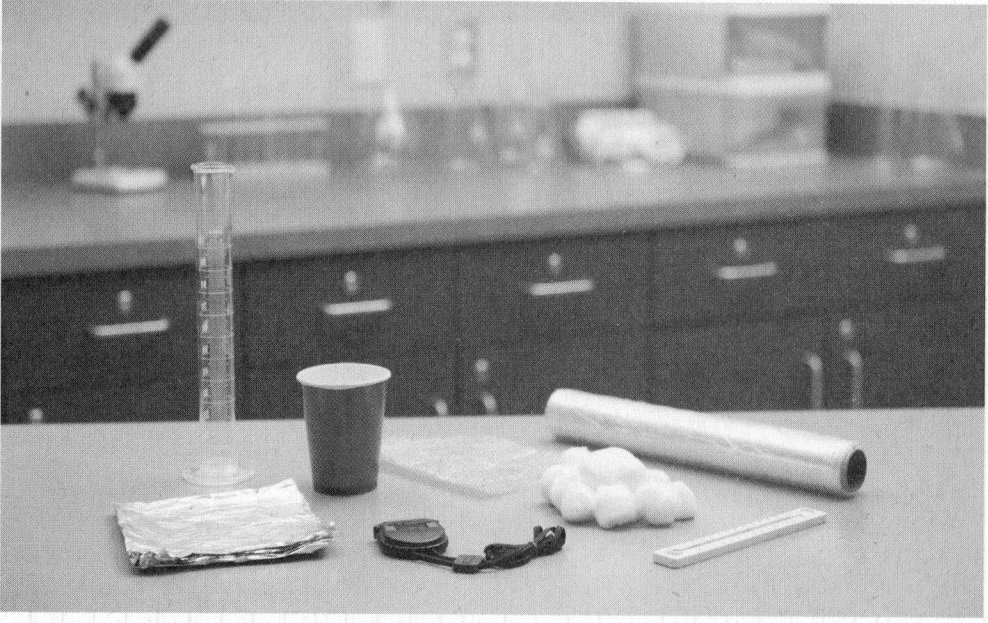

Some materials will perform better as thermal insulators than others. Testing a model will help to develop a solution.

Develop and Test a Model

Once you have determined that one or more of the solutions best meets the criteria and constraints, you need to test those solutions. In order to test solutions, you need to develop a model for each proposed solution. This model can be an actual device, a scale model, or a computer model. You also need to develop a method for testing how well the solution meets the design requirements. The test method should ensure that you obtain accurate data for comparing results.

Hands-On Lab

Design and Test an Insulated Container

You will design a device to insulate a paper cup containing ice-cold water. After you design the device, you will build a model and test it by measuring the change in water temperature over a period of 30 minutes.

The engineering problem is to design a system that minimizes the transfer of thermal energy to the water from its surroundings. In this case, the criteria and constraints include the use of available materials and completion of the design and construction of the model in the time designated by your teacher.

MATERIALS

- aluminum foil
- bubble packing
- cardboard
- cotton balls
- cotton fabric
- drinking straws
- graduated cylinder, 100 mL or larger
- ice
- paper cup
- plastic film
- rubber bands
- sheets of paper
- stopwatch or timer
- string
- thermometer
- water
- wire
- other materials provided by your teacher

Procedure and Analysis

STEP 1 With your group, brainstorm ideas for building an insulation system to minimize change in temperature of the water in the cup.

STEP 2 Evaluate the solutions that were suggested during the brainstorming session. During evaluation, you may want to eliminate some ideas. You may also want to combine parts of two or more ideas. Then build a model of the selected solution for testing.

STEP 3 Test your model by measuring 150 mL of ice-cold water into the cup and placing the cup in the model. Be careful not to include any ice in the water. Measure the temperature of the water, and record it as time zero on the data table.

STEP 4 After 5 minutes, measure and record the temperature of the water. Repeat every 5 minutes for 30 minutes.

STEP 5 What did you observe during your investigation? How do your data show that a transfer of thermal energy did or did not occur?

Thermal Energy Transfer Data

Time (min)	Temperature (°C)
0	
5	
10	
15	
20	
25	
30	

Analyze and Revise the Design

After completing the test, you need to analyze the data resulting from the test of the design solution. Compare your results with those of others in the class. Evaluate how different design solutions performed. With your group, discuss how each aspect of the design may have contributed to its success or failure.

20.  **Language SmArts** Based on your analysis, suggest some modifications to improve your container. Support your argument using evidence from your experiment and the text.

Analyze Geothermal Heat Pumps

Geothermal technology uses the transfer of thermal energy to or from the ground beneath a structure. Just a few feet below the ground's surface, the temperature is almost constant all year long. Geothermal heat pumps take advantage of the difference between the above-ground air temperature and the soil temperature below the surface to warm and cool buildings. A liquid is pumped through underground pipes. To warm a room, the pump transfers thermal energy from the liquid to the building's heating system. Then the cooled liquid flows through the pipes underground where thermal energy flows into it again before returning to the indoor heating system. For cooling, the heat pump adds thermal energy to the liquid, which is cooled underground.

21. Geothermal heat pumps require a lot less energy than traditional heating and air conditioning systems. How do the energy inputs and outputs differ between a house with a heat pump and a house with a furnace that burns fuel? Explain why using this technology could lead to a reduction of the issues associated with urban heat islands and other problems.

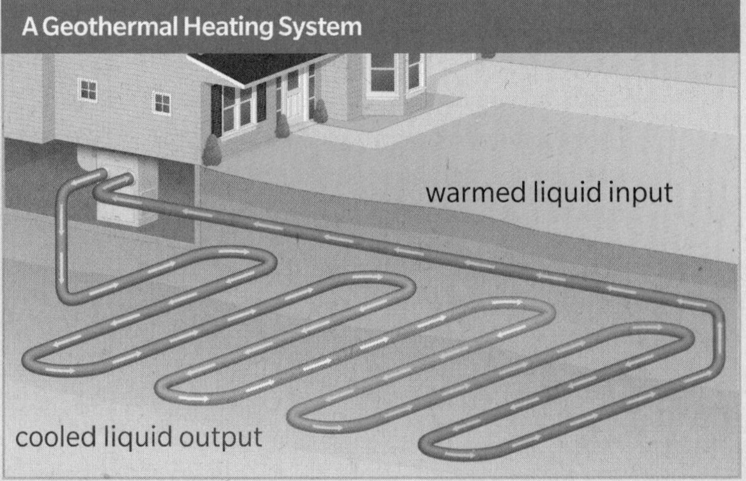

Continue Your Exploration

Name: Date:

Check out the path below or go online to choose one of the other paths shown.

Careers in Engineering

- **Hands-On Labs**
- **Maximizing Heat Transfer**
- **Propose Your Own Path**

Go online to choose one of these other paths.

Energy Conservationist

Many modern systems such as buildings, transportation networks, and lighting systems consume a lot of energy. This energy usage is expensive, consumes a large amount of natural resources, and causes pollution that contributes to global climate change. Energy conservationists work to develop solutions to reduce energy consumption. An energy conservationist may also be an engineer, an environmental scientist, or a building designer. The main goal of the job is to increase the efficiency of systems so they use less energy but still function well. To do this, the energy conservationist has to understand how energy is generated and transmitted and how it is used in the system. The best solution to the problem of energy conservation often saves money, even if it requires new equipment. Energy conservationists have to find ways to save energy in industries such as hotels, commercial properties, municipalities, and even in private homes. Then they make recommendations to solve the engineering design problem of reducing energy consumption.

An energy conservationist measures energy usage and designs ways to reduce it.

1. An energy conservationist often works as a consultant who makes recommendations that other people use to make decisions. What type of information would the energy conservationist have to consider in order to convince people that changes are a good idea?

Continue Your Exploration

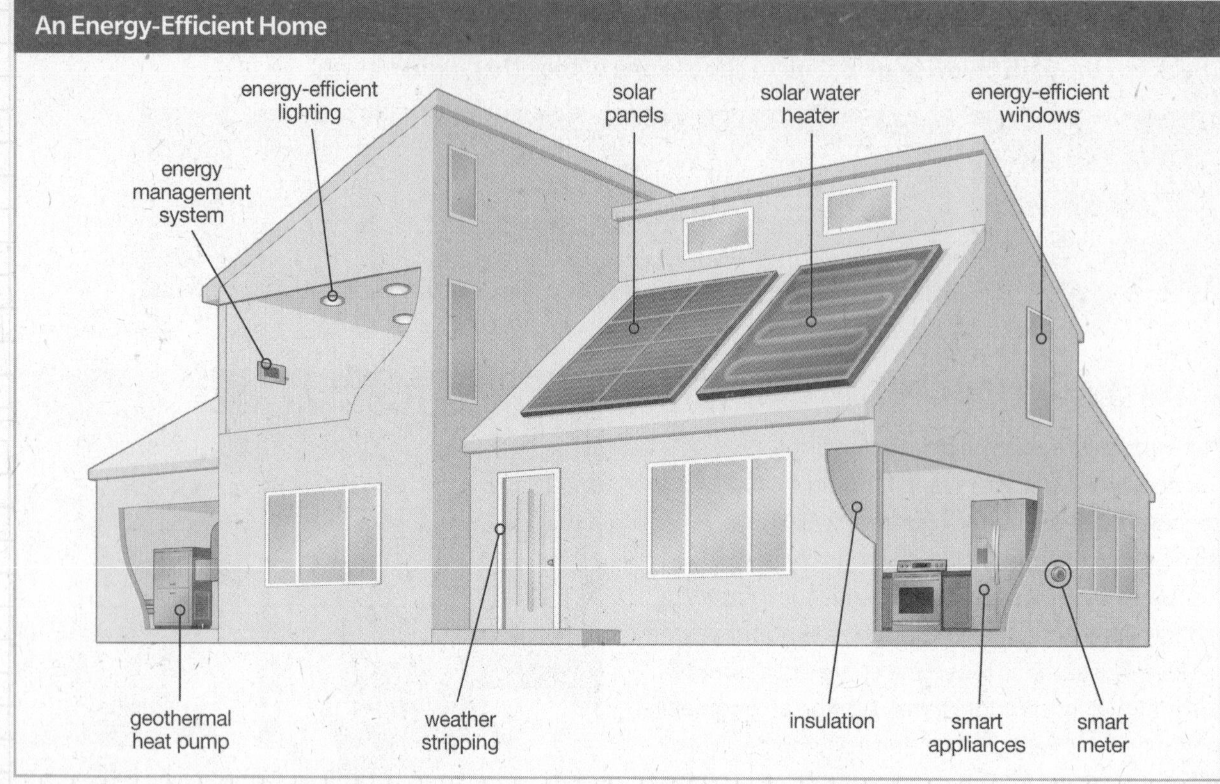

One way to improve home energy usage is to use renewable resources such as solar energy or geothermal energy and reduce fuel and electric usage. Another approach is to reduce energy use. Efficient appliances, insulation, and well-designed windows and doors reduce impacts on the environment and the costs of providing energy.

2. Which of these changes might be suggested by an energy conservationist to reduce the transfer of thermal energy to a home's surroundings? Select all that apply.

A. Add more insulation to the attic of the home.

B. Use renewable energy sources instead of fossil fuels to heat the home.

C. Install the most energy-efficient appliances available.

3. An energy conservationist studies a home and makes a suggestion that each room should have a separate thermostat instead of having one temperature control device in a central room. How could this suggestion help reduce energy usage in the home?

4. Collaborate Discuss with a group how you and your families can be "energy conservationists" in your own everyday lives. What steps do you take to make sure your use of energy is most efficient? As a group, make a poster showing things that you can do to minimize your energy use and share your ideas with the class.

Can You Explain It?

Name: Date:

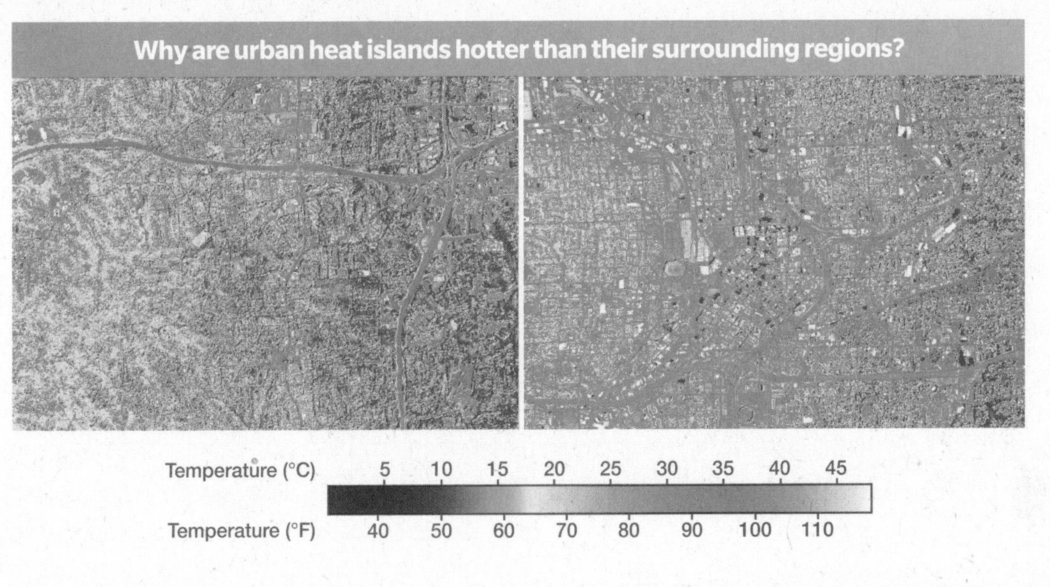

EVIDENCE NOTEBOOK

Refer to the notes in your Evidence Notebook to help you construct an explanation for the causes of urban heat islands.

1. State your claim. Make sure your claim fully explains the transfer of thermal energy within systems.

2. Summarize the evidence you have gathered to support your claim and explain your reasoning.

Checkpoints

Answer the following questions to check your understanding of the lesson.

Use the table to answer Question 3.

3. When you cook food by stir-frying, it is important to transfer thermal energy to the food as quickly as possible. Which of these metals would be the best choice for a pan intended for stir-frying vegetables?

A. aluminum

B. copper

C. stainless steel

D. tin

Thermal Conductivities of Substances	
Substance	**Thermal conductivity (W/m•K)**
Aluminum	205
Cloth (wool)	0.07
Copper	401
Polyethylene	0.42
Polystyrene foam	0.03
Stainless steel	16
Tin	67
Wood (pine)	0.12

4. Why would a light-colored roof be preferable to a dark roof in a warm, sunny area?

A. The dark-colored roof will not cool the house as quickly at nighttime.

B. The dark-colored roof absorbs more energy during the day and becomes hotter.

C. The light-colored roof absorbs more energy and keeps it from entering the house.

D. The light-colored roof cools the house faster than the dark-colored roof.

5. If you place a hot piece of metal in a container of water, thermal energy flows from the metal to the water. What happens after the metal and the water reach the same temperature?

A. The flow of thermal energy stops, and the temperature remains constant.

B. The flow of thermal energy continues and causes both substances to become warmer.

C. The flow of thermal energy reverses and causes both substances to become warmer.

D. The flow of thermal energy reverses, and the water becomes colder.

Use the diagram to answer Question 6.

6. There are two streams of liquid flowing through the heat exchanger. As these streams pass opposite sides of the tubes, thermal energy transfers from Liquid A/ Liquid B to Liquid A/ Liquid B.

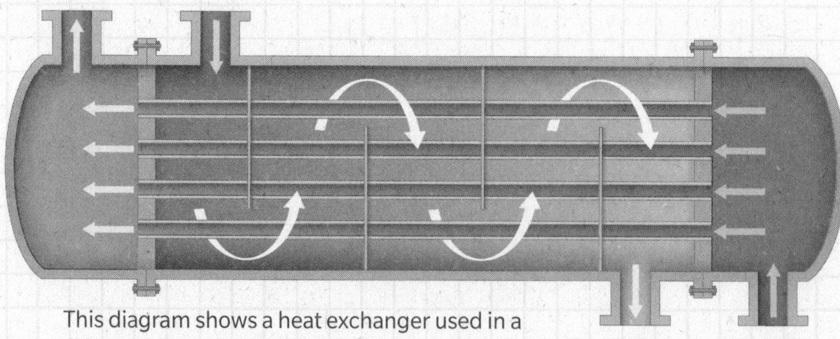

This diagram shows a heat exchanger used in a chemical processing plant. Thermal energy is transferred between the liquids flowing through the tubes in the exchanger.

Interactive Review

Complete this interactive study guide to review the lesson.

Thermal energy flows from a warmer object or substance to a cooler object or substance. The total amount of thermal energy in a system does not change unless energy transfers into or out of the system.

A. How does the flow of thermal energy in a solid object change when it is taken from a warm building out into the cold?

The amount of thermal energy that a substance or object contains depends on its temperature, composition, physical state, and mass.

B. How does the thermal energy of a pie fresh out of the oven compare to the thermal energy of a pie fresh out of the refrigerator?

Thermal conductors transfer thermal energy faster than thermal insulators.

Images/Contributor/Universal Images Group/Getty Images

C. How is a thermal mass in a building similar to a large body of water, such as a lake?

Choose one of the activities to explore how this unit connects to other topics.

☐ Environmental Science Connection

Passive Solar Design Heating and cooling a building requires a lot of energy, and it can be very expensive. Buildings designed to use the sun's energy for warmth in the winter and to minimize solar heating in the summer are becoming more popular. These passive solar buildings can greatly reduce the need for energy and heating and cooling costs.

Research the features of a passive solar building. Draw a diagram that explains how the features keep the building warm in the winter by maximizing energy transfer from the sun and keep it cool in the summer by minimizing energy transfer from the sun.

☐ Technology Connection

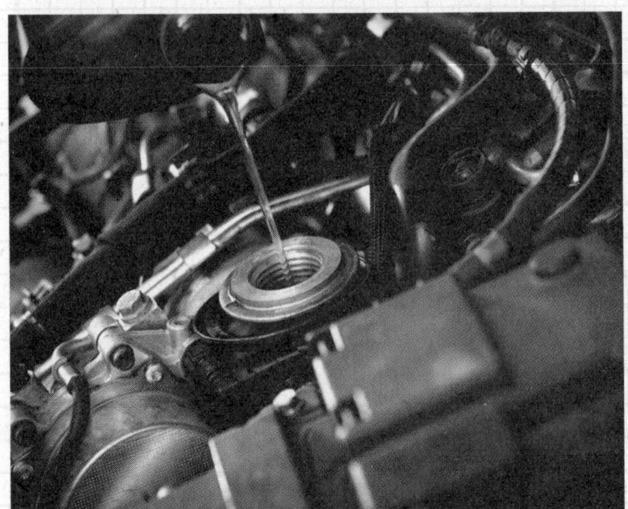

Time for an Oil Change You have probably seen service stations where people can stop in for a quick oil change in their vehicles. This is an important part of the regular maintenance service needed by all vehicles with internal combustion engines, including cars, motorcycles, and even lawnmowers. Why is changing the oil so important?

Research and write a brief report that describes how an internal combustion engine works. Explain why having clean engine oil helps make vehicles with these engines more energy efficient.

☐ Social Studies Connection

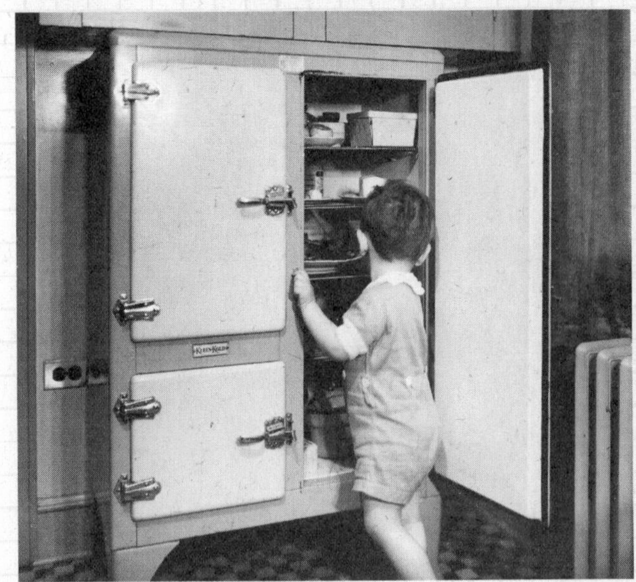

Chilling Out People often open and close refrigerator doors a dozen or more times a day without even thinking about it. We count on refrigerators to minimize thermal energy transfer and keep our food cold so it stays fresh and does not spoil. Today, most of us take the refrigerator for granted, but people did not always have easy access to fresh, cold food.

Research the history of the refrigerator. Create a timeline to show the progression from iceboxes to the modern-day refrigerator. Include key events along the way in developing this important and convenient technology.

Name: Date:

Complete this review to check your understanding of the unit.

Use the image of the fan to answer Questions 1 and 2.

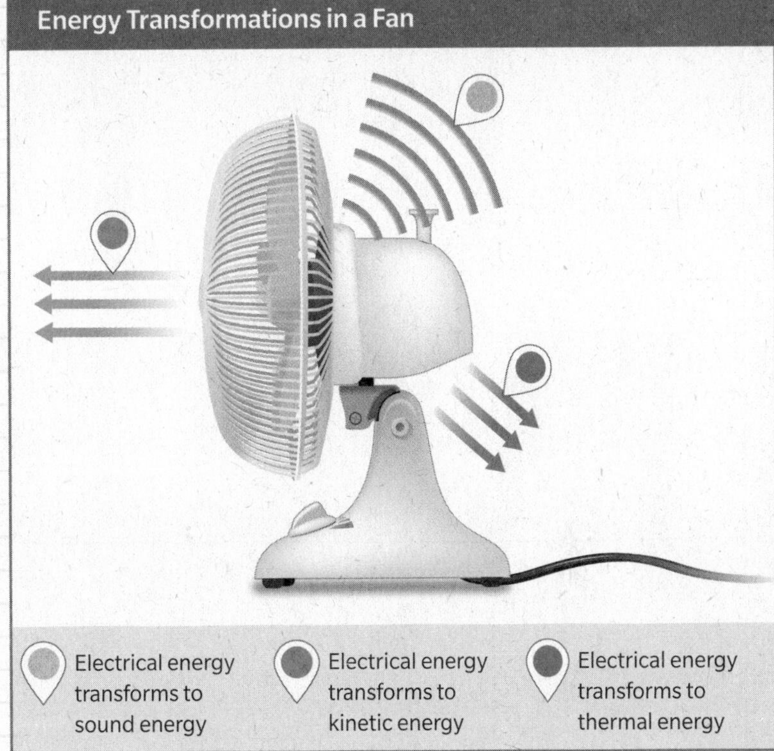

Energy Transformations in a Fan
Electrical energy transforms to sound energy
Electrical energy transforms to kinetic energy
Electrical energy transforms to thermal energy

1. In order to be more energy efficient, the fan should transform the most possible electrical energy that enters it into:
   - **A.** kinetic energy of the fan blades
   - **B.** sound energy in the fan's motor
   - **C.** thermal energy in the fan's motor
   - **D.** electromagnetic energy in the fan's blades

2. A transformation of chemical energy to electrical energy would occur if the fan were plugged into:
   - **A.** a solar-powered generator
   - **B.** a wind-powered generator
   - **C.** a hydropower generator
   - **D.** a fuel-powered generator

Use the chart to answer Questions 3 and 4.

3. Which of the materials in the thermal conductivity table would be best suited for constructing a griddle to cook items as quickly as possible?
   - **A.** tin
   - **B.** copper
   - **C.** plastic
   - **D.** nickel

4. Which material would be best suited for constructing the outer shell of a toaster to protect other surfaces from heat?
   - **A.** aluminum
   - **B.** copper
   - **C.** plastic
   - **D.** nickel

Thermal Conductivity of Materials

Material	Thermal conductivity (W/m•K)
Aluminum	205
Copper	386
Nickel	90
Plastic	0.50
Tin	65

5. Complete the table by providing examples of how each system relates to each big-picture concept.

System	Forms of energy	Transfer of energy	Transformation of energy	Scale, proporti and quantit
Roller coaster	Mechanical, kinetic, potential, electrical			
Diesel engine				
Waffle iron				

Name: **Date:**

Use the images of the fish tank and fish bowl to answer Questions 6–9.

6. Compare the thermal energy in each container if the water is the same temperature.

7. If you start with water at the same temperature in both containers without fish and add the same amount of ice to each tank, which container would cool more quickly?

8. Assume a heater is added to each container, again starting with water at the same temperature. How would the energy required to heat the containers to a new temperature differ? Explain your reasoning.

9. Suppose identical aquarium ornaments that are the same temperature, but warmer than the water, are added to each container. If the water in each container is originally the same temperature, which piece will cool more quickly? How would the overall change in water temperature differ between the two containers over time?

Use the body temperature graph to answer Questions 10–13.

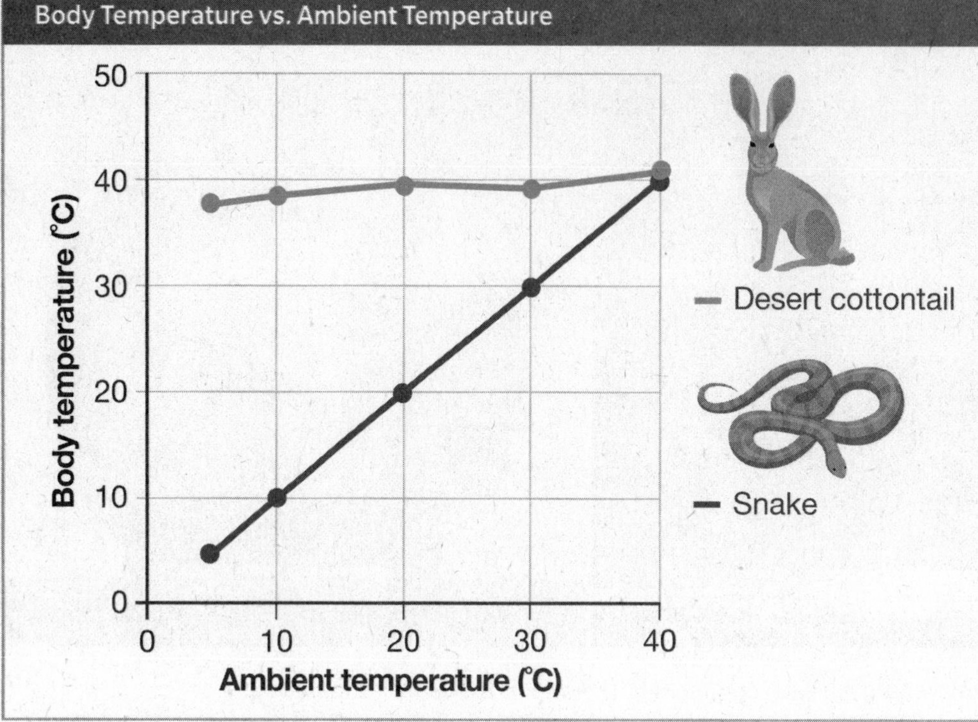

Warm-blooded animals, such as desert cottontails, tend to maintain a stable body temperature in normal environmental conditions. The body temperatures of cold-blooded animals, such as snakes, are dependent on their environment.

10. Describe the body temperatures of a desert cottontail and a snake compared to their surrounding (ambient) temperature.

11. Where does the snake get the energy to change its body temperature? Where does the energy go?

12. Snakes do not have an internal mechanism to regulate body temperature. How could a snake stay cool on a hot day?

13. Humans are able to maintain a nearly constant internal body temperature of about 37 °C even when it is very hot by perspiring. How does this process work to cool a person's body?

Name: Date:

How can you cool water faster?

Hyperthermia, or heat stroke, is a life-threatening condition of elevated body temperature. Emergency medical providers know that the best way to treat people suffering from hyperthermia is to cool them very quickly by submerging them in cold water. This lifesaving process must be performed as quickly as possible to avoid deadly complications.

You are on a team of first responders tasked with developing a first aid station by the organizing committee of a local marathon. This first aid station will need to be prepared to treat runners suffering from hyperthermia. You will have large tubs of water available, along with two different forms of ice—crushed and cubed. Which type of ice should your team use to cool the tub of water as rapidly as possible? Prepare a report for the committee that includes your recommendation of which type of ice to use.

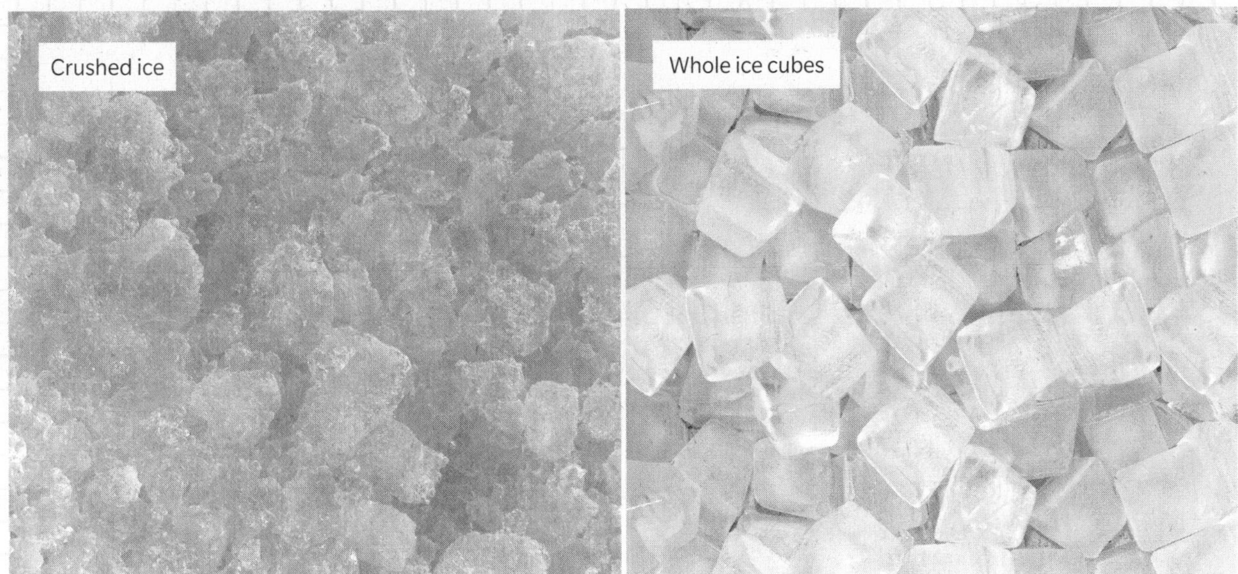
Crushed ice
Whole ice cubes

The steps below will help guide your research and recommend a solution.

Engineer It

1. **Define the Problem** What is the engineering problem you are trying to solve? Describe your criteria and constraints.

Engineer It

2. **Develop a Model** Prepare a diagram that shows how the transfer of energy occurs within the system. Describe how the problem could be modeled on a smaller scale for testing.

3. **Design an Investigation** Develop a procedure for testing the solutions to obtain measurable data. What could you use as your experimental control?

4. **Compare Solutions** Describe how each type of ice would transfer thermal energy in a large water bath. What other factors might you need to consider when selecting the best solution?

5. **Identify and Recommend a Solution** Identify which type of ice to use at the first aid station, and share your recommendation with the organizing committee.

Self-Check

	I defined the engineering problem, including the criteria and constraints.
	I developed a model representing the problem.
	I designed an investigation to meaningfully compare the solutions.
	I compared the solutions based on performance and other considerations.
	I identified and recommended a solution.

Glossary

Pronunciation Key							
Sound	**Symbol**	**Example**	**Respelling**	**Sound**	**Symbol**	**Example**	**Respelling**
ă	a	pat	PAT	ŏ	ah	bottle	BAHT'l
ā	ay	pay	PAY	ō	oh	toe	TOH
âr	air	care	KAIR	ô	aw	caught	KAWT
ä	ah	father	FAH•ther	ôr	ohr	roar	ROHR
är	ar	argue	AR•gyoo	oi	oy	noisy	NOYZ•ee
ch	ch	chase	CHAYS	o͝o	u	book	BUK
ĕ	e	pet	PET	o͞o	oo	boot	BOOT
ĕ (at end of a syllable)	eh	settee lessee	seh•TEE leh•SEE	ou	ow	pound	POWND
ĕr	ehr	merry	MEHR•ee	s	s	center	SEN•ter
ē	ee	beach	BEECH	sh	sh	cache	CASH
g	g	gas	GAS	ŭ	uh	flood	FLUHD
ĭ	i	pit	PIT	ûr	er	bird	BERD
ĭ (at end of a syllable)	ih	guitar	gih•TAR	z	z	xylophone	ZY•luh•fohn
ī	y eye (only for a complete syllable)	pie island	PY EYE•luhnd	z	z	bags	BAGZ
îr	ir	hear	HIR	zh	zh	decision	dih•SIZH •uhn
j	j	germ	JERM	ə	uh	around broken focus	uh•ROWND BROH•kuhn FOH•kuhs
k	k	kick	KIK	ər	er	winner	WIN•er
ng	ng	thing	THING	th	th	thin they	THIN THAY
ngk	ngk	bank	BANGK	w	w	one	WUHN
				wh	hw	whether	HWETH•er

A–Z

energy (EN•er•jee)
the capacity to do work (6)
energía la capacidad de realizar un trabajo

energy transfer (EN•er•jee TRANS•fer)
the movement of energy from one object or place to another (82)
transferencia de energía el movimiento de la energía de un objeto o lugar a otro

energy transformation (EN•er•jee trans•fohr•MAY•shuhn)
the process of energy changing from one form into another (85)
transformación de energía el proceso de cambio de un tipo de energía a otro

field (FEELD)
any region in which a physical force has an effect (45)
campo de fuerza cualquier región en la que se efectúa una fuerza física

heat (HEET)
the energy transferred between objects that are at different temperatures (104)
calor la transferencia de energía entre objetos que están a temperaturas diferentes

kinetic energy (kih•NET•ik EN•er•jee)
the energy of an object that is due to the object's motion (8)
energía cinética la energía de un objeto debido al movimiento del objeto

potential energy (puh•TEN•shuhl EN•er•jee)
the energy that an object has because of the position, condition, or chemical composition of the object (8)
energía potencial la energía que tiene un objeto debido a su posición, condición o composición química

system (SIS•tuhm)
a set of particles or interacting components considered to be a distinct physical entity for the purpose of study (12)
sistema un conjunto de partículas o componentes que interactúan unos con otros, el cual se considera una entidad física independiente para fines de estudio

temperature (TEM•per•uh•chur)
a measure of how hot (or cold) something is; specifically, a measure of the average kinetic energy of the particles in an object (98)
temperatura una medida de qué tan caliente (o frío) está algo; específicamente, una medida de la energía cinética promedio de las partículas de un objeto

thermal energy (THER•muhl EN•er•jee)
the total kinetic energy of a substance's particles (99)
energía térmica energía cinética total de las partículas de una sustancia

work (WERK)
the transfer of energy to an object by using a force that causes the object to move in the direction of the force (7)
trabajo la transferencia de energía a un objeto mediante una fuerza que hace que el objeto se mueva en la dirección de la fuerza

Index

Note: Italic page numbers represent illustrative material, such as figures, tables, margin elements, photographs, and illustrations. Boldface page numbers represent page numbers for definitions.

F

G

H

R

S

T

U

W